M000306513

WELLBEING, JUSTICE AND DEVELOPMENT ETHICS

The question of the meaning of progress and development is back on the political agenda. How to frame answers and search for new alternatives when socialism and liberalism no longer provide a satisfactory framework? This book introduces in an accessible way the capability approach, first articulated by Amartya Sen in the early 1980s. Written for an international audience, but rooted in the Latin American reality – a region with a history of movements for social justice – the book argues that the capability approach provides the most encompassing and promising ethical framework to date with which to construct action for improving people's wellbeing and reducing injustices in the world.

Comprehensive, practical and nuanced in its treatment of the capability approach, this highly original volume gives students, researchers and professionals in the field of development an innovative framing of the capability approach as a 'language' for action and provides specific examples of how it has made a difference.

Séverine Deneulin is Senior Lecturer in International Development, Department of Social and Policy Sciences, University of Bath, UK.

The Routledge Human Development and Capability Debates series

Series editors: Séverine Deneulin, Ortrud Leßmann and Krushil Watene

This series aims to foster multi-disciplinary discussions of contemporary issues, using the normative framework of the 'capability approach' and human development paradigm. It considers the extent to which the capability approach, and its perspective of human freedom, provides useful and innovative ways of interpreting and analysing various social realities, such as wellbeing and justice; land conflict; indigenous rights; and technological innovation.

By highlighting both the strengths and limitations of this freedom perspective, each volume provides a comprehensive, concise and jargon-free overview of a range of contemporary challenges for postgraduate students, policymakers and practitioners.

Informed by original empirical and analytical insights, the books in this series explore innovative solutions for real-world change to foster debate in the scholarly and professional communities.

We invite book proposals which engage with a variety of fields as they relate to this ethical perspective, with a preference for those which focus on key issues or topical areas of international relevance.

WELLBEING, JUSTICE AND DEVELOPMENT ETHICS

Séverine Deneulin

Routledge
Taylor & Francis Group

LONDON AND NEW YORK

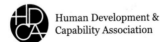

Human Development &
Capability Association

from Routledge

First published 2014
by Routledge
2 Park Square, Milton Park, Abingdon, Oxon, OX14 4RN

and by Routledge
711 Third Avenue, New York, NY 10017

Routledge is an imprint of the Taylor & Francis Group, an informa business

© 2014 Séverine Deneulin

British Library Cataloguing in Publication Data
A catalogue record for this book is available from the British Library

Library of Congress Cataloging-in-Publication Data
Deneulin, Séverine, 1974–
    Wellbeing, justice and development ethics / Séverine Deneulin.
        pages cm. – (The routledge human development and capability
        debates)
        Includes bibliographical references and index.
    1. Economic development–Moral and ethical aspects. 2. Social
justice. 3. Welfare economics. 4. Economic development–Social
aspects–Latin America. 5. Social justice–Latin America. 6. Welfare
economics–Latin America. I. Title.
    HD75.D454 2014
    174'.4--dc23   2013032807

ISBN13: 978-0-415-72023-6 (hbk)
ISBN13: 978-0-415-72024-3 (pbk)
ISBN13: 978-1-315-86709-0 (ebk)

Typeset in Bembo by
Keystroke, Station Road, Codsall, Wolverhampton

Combining conceptual analysis and case studies, this book shows that poor people, their capabilities and agency, must be the foundations of the kind of thinking about well-being and justice that will prepare us for a 'post-development' world, in which the artificial constructs of North and South are replaced by the much more tangible and universal divides between haves and have-nots.

Duncan Green, Oxfam International

Within the world of development policy, there has been a very well-justified push for the so-called 'evidence-based policy making'. However, this entails the risk of creating an illusion of 'objectivity', which hides the system of ethical values behind specific prescriptions. This book does a great job of providing a solid normative framework for policy: widening the set of effective options people have to live the life they have reason to value. Many of the practical implications of such a framework are discussed in this work, which hopefully will become a reference for anyone engaged in the difficult task of policy advice.

*Luis F. Lopez-Calva, Lead Economist and Regional Poverty Advisor,
Europe and Central Asia Region, World Bank*

CONTENTS

TABLES

ACKNOWLEDGEMENTS

This book is the result of more than a decade of friendships and exchange of ideas with members of the Human Development and Capability Association (HDCA). It was at St Edmund's College in Cambridge (UK) that scattered individuals working on the capability approach met for the first time in June 2001 to share their research. Amartya Sen was the main guest speaker. We enjoyed it so much that we decided to hold another conference at the same place the following year, this time with Martha Nussbaum. The number of participants doubled and we decided to meet again in Pavia (Italy) the following year. The informal gathering of about 70 individuals in 2001 led to the formation of an academic association in 2004. HDCA now counts more than 700 members in more than 70 countries.

This book has benefited from discussions over the years with Frances Stewart, Sabina Alkire, Jean-Luc Dubois, Ingrid Robeyns, Elaine Unterhalter, Mozaffar Qizilbash, Des Gasper, Flavio Comim, Solava Ibrahim, Melanie Walker, Mario Biggeri, Enrica Chiappero-Martinetti, Jean-François Trani and many other HDCA members. I am very grateful to Ann Mitchell and Areli Valencia for allowing me to use their research and for their comments on Chapter 4, and to Ilse Oosterlaken, Augusto Zampini, Andrea Baertl, Krushil Watene and Dana Bates for commenting on the manuscript. And, last but not least, I am greatly indebted to the students of the MSc in Wellbeing and International Development at the University of Bath in the UK and the MSc in International Cooperation and Development at the University of Bethlehem in the Occupied Palestinian Territories. Since 2007, they have brought me a constant supply of fresh energy to write and teach on the capability approach.

Chapter 1 contains material from 'Ethics and Development: An Introduction from the Perspective of the Capability Approach', *Geography Compass*, 2013, 7(3): 217–27; Chapter 3 contains material from 'Recovering Nussbaum's Aristotelian Roots', *International Journal of Social Economics*, 2013, 40(7): 624–32. I thank Wiley-Blackwell and Emerald Group Publishing for their kind permission to reproduce some parts of these articles. The basic argument of this book was first set out in a Festschrift written for Richard Jolly entitled 'Constructing new policy narratives: The capability approach as normative language', which is due to be published by Oxford University Press in a volume edited by Frances Stewart and Giovanni Andrea Cornia.

INTRODUCTION

Background

'Another world is possible'. This was the motto of the first World Social Forum in Porto Alegre in Brazil in 2001. Since then, discontent with the way economic, social and political relations are structured, whether at the local, national or global level, has intensified in many parts of the world. From deforestation and logging in the Philippines, to land being taken from farmers to make room for mining activities in India, Myanmar, Peru, Ecuador or Madagascar, to the irresponsible financial speculation and the bank bailouts with taxpayers' money, to tax dodging and financial offshore centres, the list of grievances worldwide is endless. Despite their geographical spread, these grievances have a common thread: they express dissatisfaction with economic, political and social arrangements which are perceived to benefit a privileged minority disregarding the majority of the population as well as the shared natural environment in which all, privileged or not, live.

At the global level, inequality has increased dramatically over the last 200 years. The global Gini coefficient was estimated to have risen from 0.43 in 1820 to reach 0.707 in 2002 – the coefficient is 0 when all assets are shared equally and 1 when owned by one person. When financial assets, property and savings were added to income, the coefficient was estimated at 0.899 in 2000.[1] In the United Kingdom, the gap between average pay and high pay has increased to such a level that in 2012, the average executive salary was 185 times that of the average salary.[2] Globally in 2012, one out of eight people in the world suffered from hunger, despite a global capacity to feed everyone.[3] Norway, the country currently enjoying the highest level of development as measured by life expectancy, schooling and income, currently consumes more than 3.1 times what would be required for global environmental sustainability.[4]

Against this picture of gloom, searches for new ways of relating to each other in economic and social exchanges are springing up. In France, local communities are increasingly forming producer or consumer associations or cooperatives so as to guarantee a fairer price to all and encourage sustainable farming methods (Pelenc et al. 2013). In Mexico, the Zapatistas are creating new forms of political relations in autonomous communities where hierarchy is replaced by rotating power and decisions oriented at more egalitarian relations between people and greater respect for the environment (Stahler-Sholk 2007). At the global level, *Via Campesina* is a network of more than 150 national farmers' organizations over five continents to promote small-scale sustainable agriculture and influence national and international agriculture-related policy to guarantee food sovereignty and the rights to food and to land (Borras 2010, Desmarais 2008, Martinez-Torres and Rosset 2010).

In parallel to these initiatives aimed at transforming structures of production and consumption in view of the wellbeing of all and the future of the planet, there are also initiatives aimed at transforming the meaning of progress, from material growth to human growth. Progress is not about what an economy produces or consumes, in other words about the growth of a country's Gross Domestic Product (GDP), but about what these production and consumption activities do to people and their environment. The United Nations Development Programme (UNDP) was a global trendsetter in the early 1990s with its Human Development Index to measure the wealth of nations by indicators of health, education and living standards (UNDP 2010). In 2007, the Organization for Economic Co-operation and Development (OECD) launched its 'Measuring the Progress of Societies Initiative' to develop new indicators of progress to include work–life balance, education, environmental protection, health and living conditions. Its Better Life Index seeks to replace GDP growth as a measure of progress.[5] The Himalayan Kingdom of Bhutan measures its progress with a Gross National Happiness Index, which includes indicators related to mental health, spirituality, quality of relationships and culture.[6] The Office for National Statistics in the UK is currently computing a National Wellbeing Index to measure how well the country is doing in various domains such as life satisfaction, employment, environment, economic security and health.[7]

All the above initiatives, whether aimed at transforming or creating new economic, social and political structures or at measuring progress differently, are set against a rejection of the two grand narratives which have divided the world for most of the twentieth century and have provided so far a framework which people could draw on to construct their realities and their future. Socialism, with its promise of an all-encompassing state as the guarantor of wellbeing, had denied people a fundamental aspect of their humanity: their agency or ability to shape their own lives and the world around them. Liberalism, with its promise of an all-encompassing individual freedom as the guarantor of wellbeing, denied people another fundamental aspect of their humanity: their interrelatedness or the quality of their shared existence. The reality of the world today calls for a new framework which people could draw on to shape their social and political action, while respecting their agency and providing support for their wellbeing in a shared social, political and economic environment.

Aims

The aim of this book is to introduce in an accessible way a framework which may provide us with the necessary conceptual tools to help frame social and political action and transform current institutional arrangements on the basis of these two fundamental aspects of our humanity: agency and wellbeing, for humans to decide what it means to live well in relation to each other, and how to do so. The book argues that the capability approach provides such a framework, which could help transform or create different social, economic and political arrangements from the ones which deepen inequality, undermine people's opportunities to live well and destroy the environment.

The concept of capability first appeared in 1979 in Amartya Sen's Tanner Lecture, 'Equality of What?' (Sen 1980). If we are concerned about equality, Sen argued, then the most appropriate space to assess it is not that of income or resources but that of 'capabilites', or opportunities people have to reach certain beings and doings. Measuring inequality in terms of income is not to be discarded but income is only a means to other ends such as buying food to be healthy, a house to be sheltered and be hospitable to others, or books to be educated and informed. By focusing on the means – income – we risk losing sight of the end – the type of lives that we are living and how well we are or do.

The capability approach is hence an approach to assess equality from the perspective of capabilities. The success of, for example, an employment policy which has introduced a minimum wage, is to be assessed not according to whether the policy has increased national income but whether it has increased people's capabilities, or opportunities they have to be or do what they have reason to value, such as opportunities to pursue knowledge, participate in the life of the community, appreciate beauty, engage in meaningful work, be healthy, move freely from place to place, be adequately nourished, play and rest, to name a few of what people may have reason to value being or doing. According to this approach, a state of affairs in which people are able to do or be what they have reason to value, is better than another state in which they are not able to achieve valuable beings or doings. By providing such an evaluation framework, the capability approach offers a horizon which people can look at when they engage in social and political action in their striving for living well on a shared planet.

This book provides a critical overview of what the capability approach is, and discusses its revolutionary nature. It introduces the capability approach as a normative language for social and political action. It is a language because it contains some basic recurrent words and grammar – wellbeing, capabilities, functionings, agency, public reasoning – and it is normative because the words are used to construct moral judgements. Should the Peruvian government give agro-business exporters a special tax regime? Should the Panamanian government invest financial resources in building hydroelectric dams on its rivers? Should the Argentinian government have an expansionary monetary policy? The capability approach is concerned with these policy questions and, as the book will tease out, it can help provide some outline answers.

As a normative language, the capability approach is relevant for making moral judgements not only at the policy but also at the individual level. In his Nobel Lecture for the Prize of Economics, Gary Becker told his audience that he had had the insight of applying utilitarian economic theory to crime, one area for which he was awarded the Nobel Prize, when he arrived late for an oral examination and had to decide whether to park in a paying car park and arrive late, or park illegally and arrive on time (Becker 1993). He calculated the probability of getting fined, compared the cost of the fine with that of the parking and that of arriving late at the examination, and decided to park illegally. Using the capability approach would have led to a rather different moral judgement and decision. In contrast to Becker's approach, Sen's approach would use information about agency, or the pursuit of goals one has reason to value, and people's capabilities. Acting in view of respecting the law (assuming that respect for the rule of law is a goal one has reason to value) and therefore paying for parking in the car park, is as relevant as information in the decision process as the probability of being fined or the penalty of arriving late for an examination. Or assuming the parking space available near the examination place was a disabled parking, considerations about the capability of other people to go from place to place would also enter in the decision-making process.

As a normative language, which provides some basic words and grammar, the book presents the capability approach as versatile. How its keywords are combined and which words are important is context-dependent. Each context of analysis will yield different uses and interpretations. When used in the fields of education, health or disability, when discussed in the disciplines of economics, philosophy, sociology, law, theology or engineering (such as technology design), when used as an evaluation framework for assessing the situation of women in Africa, unemployed young people in Germany or indigenous peoples in the Andes, the capability approach, so the book argues, will be used and interpreted differently. The keywords and grammar remain the same, but the combination of these will vary according to the contexts in which the normative language is spoken, the audience to which it is addressed and the speakers who speak the sentences and narrate the socio-economic analysis.

Scope

It has been more than thirty years since Sen introduced the word 'capability' into the social sciences. It was addressed to economists who used utility as a measure for assessing states of affairs and to philosophers who used Rawls's primary goods as relevant information for constructing a theory of justice. The word took off and spread more widely in the 1990s to other audiences, due in part to the collaboration with classicist and philosopher Martha Nussbaum and their joint project at the World Institute for Development Economics Research in Helsinki on assessing quality of life (which led to the publication in 1993 of the edited volume by Nussbaum and Sen, *The Quality of Life*, published by Clarendon Press). Both Sen and Nussbaum wrote prolifically in the 1980s and 1990s about assessing states of affairs and making moral judgements and decisions from the perspective of capabilities. Sen vowed in 1979 'not to desist from doing some propaganda on its behalf' (Sen 1980: 197), and he has indeed not desisted since then.

The word 'capability' has now taken a life of its own, despite its unattractiveness and the difficulty of translating it in other languages.[8] In the early 2000s, a growing number of young academics conducted their doctoral research on the capability approach, and the first international conference on the capability approach was held in June 2001 in Cambridge, UK, and has been held annually ever since in various locations worldwide. In 2004 the Human Development and Capability Association (HDCA) was formed to advance research on the capability approach and promote its use in economic and social analysis and public decision-making.

The writings on the capability approach are now numbering in the hundreds if not the thousands. An academic journal, the *Journal of Human Development and Capabilities*, is entirely dedicated to publishing papers which engage with the approach. One may therefore wonder about the need for yet another publication on the topic. A first reason for this book is that the material which presents the approach to a non-academic audience remains limited. In 2009, a textbook entitled *An Introduction the Human Development and Capability Approach* (Deneulin 2009) was written by various members of HDCA to offer a pedagogical and accessible introduction to a student audience. In 2011, Martha Nussbaum wrote *Creating Capabilities* for a non-research oriented audience. This book similarly aims at being an accessible introduction, but with a different angle. It seeks to articulate more explicitly how the capability approach is an alternative normative language with which to frame decisions and actions, and how it offers a distinctive analysis of situations. The book aims at stimulating critical reflection on current economic and social practices and at providing a language with which to modify them within the horizon of human wellbeing, agency and just relations between people and the environment. Thus, in addition to being a presentation of what the capability approach is, the book is decision and action focused. It seeks to combine theoretical inquiry with empirical search for new economic and social practices. The question which underpins all the chapters is: how can the capability approach help us frame decisions and actions so that the reality in which we live can be closer to a situation where each person, living and to come, has opportunities to live a fulfilling human life?

A second reason for this book is that the capability approach has grown into a set of different directions over the three decades of its existence. Some see it only as a framework for assessing states of affairs; others see it as a partial theory of justice. Some see it as an exaltation of individual freedom and choice, and criticize it for not paying attention to oppressive social structures; others see it as a liberating force from oppression. This book seeks to clarify these different interpretations. It presents the capability approach not as a dogmatic set of truths which one has to adhere to in order to be faithful to it but as a flexible normative language, with some defining words and grammar, which leaves speakers free to elaborate their own analyses and responses to the reality to which they speak. The book will be mainly rooted in the Latin American reality but the reach of its argument has implications far beyond the Latin American continent.

Structure

The first chapter discusses why development, understood as the set of economic, social, cultural and political processes oriented towards improving people's lives, requires a critical reflection about the meaning of wellbeing or living well and the means to pursue it. The ethical question of how one should live, as people in relationship with each other and the environment, is fundamental to development. With concrete policy examples, the chapter shows how answering the fundamental ethical question has been, and continues to be, a matter of intense disagreement. How to weigh the costs and benefits of different policy options? How to negotiate divergent visions of what living a 'better' human life is about? How to value the environment? How to exercise power?

The second chapter introduces the capability approach as a normative language and the distinctive perspective it brings. It focuses on its defining words of wellbeing, capability, functioning and agency, and its grammar of public reasoning to structure these keywords. It examines the capability space as an alternative evaluation space and engages with other approaches to wellbeing in the social sciences. It argues that there is no single authoritative interpretation of the capability approach and that this plurality of interpretations is one of the capability approach's greatest strengths and in tune with its agency focus. The chapter highlights two areas of interpretative differences in relation to its purpose and conception of the person.

The third chapter links the capability approach to theories of justice. From an approach for assessing states of affairs in the 1980s, it is now moving towards being a partial theory of justice and offering a framework with which to transform unjust situations. The chapter describes how the capability approach enables the articulation, at the conceptual level, of practical struggles for justice. On the basis of a social movement in Ecuador, the chapter argues that a capability-based view of justice needs to include more than capabilities as the informational basis of justice. It should include the quality of economic, social and political relations people have with each other and the natural environment.

On the basis of two selected case studies from Argentina and Peru, the fourth chapter discusses how the capability approach can concretely provide a language for imagining and creating new economic, social and political realities. For each case, it will show how the language can be used to assess a specific reality, and how such assessment on the basis of people's capabilities and quality of social, economic and political relations can help generate social and political action to transform existing relations so that people may live better lives in a shared natural environment.

The fifth chapter discusses how the capability approach is an encompassing normative language, which can borrow from other normative frameworks. It argues that, like any language, it has to be nurtured within relationships and spoken through concrete practices, without which a language does not survive. The chapter examines in particular the formation of agents who act to transform economic, social and political realities so that they have more opportunities to be or do what they have reason to value. It illustrates how agents are formed through relationships in the case of a local social movement in the Peruvian Andes.

The book concludes by summarizing its argument. A just society, where each person is able to live well in relation to others and in a shared natural environment, remains a vision always in the making and unmaking precisely because it respects human agency.

Notes

1 Data from a UNICEF report entitled 'Global inequality: Beyond the bottom billion' at http://www.childimpact.unicef-irc.org/en/desk-reviews/global-inequality.
2 Data from the High Pay Centre at http://www.highpaycentre.org.
3 See data from https://www.wfp.org/hunger/stats and the FAO Report on the State of the World Food Insecurity 2012 at http://www.fao.org/publications/sofi/en.
4 This estimation is based on the ecological footprint of consumption, which measures the area of land and sea needed to regenerate the resources that a country consumes (UNDP 2010: 65).
5 See http://www.oecdbetterlifeindex.org.
6 See http://www.grossnationalhappiness.com.
7 See http://www.ons.gov.uk/ons/guide-method/user-guidance/well-being/index.html.
8 Sen (1993: 30) confessed that '[c]apability is not an awfully attractive word', and that a 'nicer word could have been chosen'.

1

DEVELOPMENT AND ETHICS

A development story from Peru

The Ica valley is a semi-arid coastal area about 300 km south of Lima. What has unravelled there in the last 25 years poignantly illustrates how decisions taken at different moments construct a certain reality with deep implications for people's lives and the environment.[1] The development story of the Ica valley highlights that the types of normative frameworks people use for individual and collective decision-making have a considerable impact on the material reality of the world.

Until the early 1990s, the Ica valley was among the regions in Peru with the lowest per capita income. The majority of the population was making a living out of small-scale agriculture. Things took a different turn when the Peruvian government, led by Fujimori, embraced the liberalization policies which characterized the Latin American macro-environment during the 1990s. Domestic markets, including the agricultural sector, opened to foreign investment. The government gave incentives for the cultivation of export crops, granted agro-businesses a special tax regime and exempted some products from import tax.

nation building?

Given this new context, farmers and agro-businesses in the Ica valley progressively switched from cotton cultivation to an all-year production of asparagus as the latter crop had become much more lucrative. The area cultivated for asparagus grew from four hectares in 1986 to 9,610 hectares in 2009. Today, Peru is the largest exporter of fresh asparagus in the world and the Ica valley produces 95 per cent of Peru's asparagus. Approximately

40 per cent of the working population of the Ica region is employed in the asparagus industry. The other major export business is in grapes, which covers about 6,000 hectares in the valley. There is near full employment and salaries are reported to be sufficient to live decently.[2] These benefits need, however, to be put in perspective. The retail value of fresh Peruvian asparagus in the UK is estimated at £55 million each year, but its street value in Ica is only £1.54 million. This suggests that the few who have benefited most from the asparagus boom have been the agro-exporters, brokers and supermarkets, not the farmers.[3]

But there is another side to this success story. The decision to give incentives to expand export agro-businesses may well have brought large income and employment benefits; it has also led to significant costs. This export-led agriculture is highly water intensive and the aquifers of this semi-arid region are running low – the region has an average rainfall of less than 1 mm per year. It is estimated that, at current rates of exploitation, a third of the city's supplies will dry in the next 25 years. In 2009, due to water shortages and poor water and sanitation infrastructure, some families in the valley were already limited to 10 litres of water per day while the World Health Organization recommends 50 litres per person per day to meet health standards. Large agro-businesses have the financial means to dig deeper wells but medium- and small-scale farmers have to use superficial water, which is running scarce. For them, continuing to cultivate asparagus has become difficult, and shifting to other crops is no longer profitable enough to make a living. Moreover, the overexploitation of water down the valley is creating water problems higher up in the Andes. Indigenous communities have to cope with water contamination and limited water supply created by the asparagus boom, forcing some of them to migrate to the valley and become temporary agricultural migrant workers to survive.

The development narrative of the Ica valley tells a story of uneven distribution of costs and benefits. On the one hand, the policy decisions to liberalize markets and support export-oriented agriculture have led to more opportunities for employment for some. On the other, if agriculture remains water intensive and if no strong measures are taken to regulate water use, people who live in the valley will be forced in the long run to migrate when water runs out. And indigenous people who live in the mountains are affected too by the water shortages down in the valley, and have fewer opportunities to sustain their way of living.

This state of affairs need not have been so. The story of the Ica valley is not one of natural laws but of human decisions taken over the last 30 years: the Peruvian government's decision to support export-oriented agriculture made investment in the asparagus industry very lucrative; the World Bank (the International Finance Corporation is the biggest investor in the asparagus sector in the Ica valley) put pressure on the Peruvian government to encourage export-led agro-businesses; Western consumers demand to eat asparagus all year round; government officials have not legislated water regulation and have allowed agro-businesses to dig wells at unsustainable rates; and where legislation exists, they have been lax at enforcing it.[4]

Each actor in the story could have made other decisions: the government of Peru could have resisted pressures from international institutions and promoted small-scale sustainable farming instead of export-oriented agriculture; Western consumers – the US, the Netherlands and the UK are the three largest markets for Peruvian asparagus – could have chosen not to demand asparagus when out of season in their countries; agro-businesses could have included in their objective of maximizing profits the objective of sustainable water use or could have invested elsewhere in Peru where water was more abundant;[5] local farmers could have been more creative in developing a system of production and consumption outside the pricing of international commodity markets, or could have resisted the transformation of the agricultural structure of the region; Peruvian citizens could have held local government accountable to ensure the respect of water regulation legislation and to expose corruption; the Peruvian government could have exercised greater control and coordination of economic activities; local government officials could have resisted bribes to grant illegal water use to businesses.

These decisions that were taken, or not taken, have landed the people in the Ica valley in a situation that cannot be changed through individual action. No farmer, no Peruvian citizen, no government official, no agro-business manager acting alone can change the plot of the above development story. Bringing the productive structure of the Ica valley in harmony with sustainable water use depends on collective action to create the necessary economic and political institutional environment for this to happen. The story of the Ica valley does not only point to the urgency of linking economic activities to environmental control and water management regulation, it also points to the urgency of reclaiming the public space to deliberate about what kind of economic and political structures best ensure the well-being of all in a shared natural environment. The export-oriented agriculture and the asparagus boom in the Ica valley have increased the region's income and given people more opportunities for decent housing, education and travel, among other things. But the consequent increase in water use has not been regulated in a way which ensures the future of life in the valley. The story invites us to reconsider the ends and means of 'development'.

Development: ends and means

Etymologically, development is the growth of something from one state to another. An acorn grows into an oak tree, which could be seen as its natural end. Societies were similarly thought to 'develop' or grow from one state into another, from an initial state to a 'natural' end. In Walter Rostow's *Stages of Economic Growth*, written in the 1950s, societies were said to develop from a primitive to an agricultural stage, then to an industrial stage and then to mass consumption societies, their final end. This discussion may perhaps appear simplistic but the question of the meaning of development or the end societies should grow into, has considerable implications for policy, and people's lives and the environment. If societies are to develop and grow into some end, how is that end determined? Is there a 'natural end' derived from human nature? Is that end specific to each society?

The word 'development' is commonly said to have entered the social sciences vocabulary after the end of the Second World War, at the start of the decolonization era when the newly independent colonies embarked on the project of modelling their societies to that of their previous colonizers (Sachs 1992). It is in the 1960s that the multi-disciplinary field of inquiry known as development studies was established to facilitate the processes of transformation from colonies to independent countries. But as such, the development project started well before the decolonization era and has its roots in the idea of progress that accompanied technological innovation in the late eighteenth century. It had first an economic dimension and then a social one to counter the human costs of the rapid growth of economic output during the Industrial Revolution.

Ever since its first uses in the social sciences, the meaning of development has been contested among people and organizations from different professional, geographical and cultural backgrounds. To some, it has meant technological innovation, to others it has meant increases in national production or income, reduction of the number of people living below the poverty line, satisfaction of basic needs, protection of human rights, or respect for cultures and their values and traditions, and many other things.[6] What these contested meanings show is that what counts as 'development' is closely connected to what counts as 'living well' or 'living better lives'.

In Latin America, it is arguably the conflicts surrounding extractive activities on indigenous peoples' land which express most strikingly the disputed meaning of development and what it is to live well. Many Latin American countries are resource rich and obtain a large share of government revenues from the extractive industry: copper in Chile, gas in Bolivia, oil in Ecuador, oil in Venezuela, timber and minerals in Brazil, oil in Colombia.[7]

But a large part of these natural resources are found on land, which has been occupied for centuries by indigenous peoples.[8] For the governments of the states in which they live, the land is a natural resource that can be used to generate economic and social benefits. Development is understood as the generation of revenues from natural resource extraction as a means to create the conditions for people to live well. In contrast, for many of the people who live on resource-rich land, the land is something which humans are part of, and which is to be respected in the same way as human life is. They understand development as living in harmony with the natural environment and not exploiting it beyond its capacity for self-regeneration. This conflict regarding the ends and means of development does not, however, play out in a simplistic way between two antagonist groups but in very complex ways, as the case of Ecuador illustrates.

The Yasuní National Park in the Amazon Basin is one of the world's most biodiverse places and hosts several indigenous communities, some of them still uncontacted (Finer *et al.* 2009). However, it is also rich in oil. The fields of the Ishpingo-Tambococha-Tiputini territory (known as ITT) contain about a fifth of Ecuador's overall oil reserves and have an estimated value of US$720 million a year (Rival 2010: 358). Since the mid-1990s, scientists, together with indigenous and environmental organizations, have been putting pressure on the Ecuadorian government to preserve the complex and rich ecosystem of the region. They proposed a plan to leave the oil under-ground and ask the international community for monetary compensation in exchange. This would mean cash into the government revenues to finance social services, an opportunity for Western countries to show their commit-ment to environmental protection, and the protection of biodiversity.

In 2007, the newly elected president of Ecuador, Rafael Correa, declared that his government would not exploit the oil of the ITT territory. A compensation fund was established – the compensation was calculated on the price of the overall carbon emissions that would have been generated by the oil extraction (Rival 2010: 361). Several European governments pledged to participate and the UNDP was set to administer it. However, in 2010, the Ecuadorian government changed its views on how to improve people's lives. Correa denounced the compensation fund he had helped set up as a breach of national sovereignty and new form of colonialism (Rival 2012: 162). Even among the supporters of the ITT initiative, there was disagree-ment about who was to administer the fund and how to manage it (Rival 2012: 165–6). These conflicts have meant that the ITT initiative and the plans to leave the oil underground are currently under threat.[9]

This contestation of the meaning of development and how to improve people's lives is further illustrated at the level of Ecuadorian national policy.

In September 2008, as a result of decades of political pressure from indigenous organizations to have their specific way of life recognized by the state (Radcliffe 2012), voters approved a new constitution by referendum, which commits the Ecuadorian government to establish an economic, social and political system oriented towards the realization of *buen vivir*, or 'living well', understood in terms of harmonious relations between people and nature.[10] This includes the guaranteeing of all economic, social, political and civil rights as well as the right of Nature.

In the next 25 years, the government aims to replace an economy based on the extraction of natural resources with one based on bio-knowledge. A national plan and a series of targets have been designed to achieve that goal.[11] However, the new constitution also stipulates that the ban on drilling in the Yasuní–ITT fields can be revoked by the president for the sake of national interests, provided Congress approves. Despite its rhetoric, Correa's government is increasing its extractive activities,[12] and concerns have been expressed about human rights violations (Bebbington and Bebbington-Humphreys 2011).[13]

Two pictures, one by the government and one by the Confederation of Kichwa Peoples of Ecuador, ECUARUNARI, illustrate this conflict about the end that societies should strive for and the means to achieve it. In a government publication for distribution in secondary schools and which contains cartoons about the development of Ecuador, one picture shows protestors against mining who are blocking access to health services. The picture suggests that, if correctly managed, mining and government collaboration with foreign mining companies can be a source of employment and social investment (Moore and Velazquez 2012: 124). On the other hand, ECUARUNARI is campaigning with a picture which shows a bulldozer coming to erase a village to make way for a mining project. The man in the bulldozer says to a farmer: 'You are poor. Sell me your land and water so that you will get money', to which the farmer responds: 'When the money will be gone, I shall have no water and no land.' To which the man in the bulldozer replies: 'Uneducated!'[14]

Do these two pictures present two different visions of development and what it means to live well? Can these views be reconciled and an agreement found? How can we know if one view is 'better' than another? Whose views within these organizations prevail? These questions lie at the heart of development ethics.

Development ethics

Reflection on the meaning of development is not new. Socialist thinkers like St Simon and Marx, and spiritual and religious leaders like Gandhi and Pope Leon XIII, already objected more than a century ago to the commodification of labour and the submission of human life to the financial objective of profit-making. Gandhi especially condemned the colonial underpinnings of economic development and its reliance on labour and resource exploitation in the colonies. It is, however, not before the end of colonization, with the emergence of development studies as a multi-disciplinary field of academic inquiry, that development ethics, defined as a critical ethical reflection on the meaning of development, became a specialist subject. The works of American development planner Denis Goulet were the first contributions to this 'new discipline' (Goulet 1997).[15]

The purpose of development, Goulet argued, was not more technology or greater wealth, but enabling people to become more human (Goulet 1971). The task of development ethics, he wrote,

> is to assure that the painful changes launched under the banner of development do not result in antidevelopment, which destroys cultures and individuals and exacts undue sacrifices in suffering and societal wellbeing – all in the name of profit, some absolutized ideology, or a supposed efficiency imperative.
>
> *(Goulet 1997: 1169)*

Goulet (1995: 8) identified four areas constitutive of development ethics:

> 1) Debates over goals: economic growth, basic needs, cultural survival, ecological balance, transfers of power from one class to another; 2) Divergent notions of power, legitimacy, authority, governance, competing political systems; 3) Competition over resources and over rules of access to resources, competing economic systems; and 4) Pervasive conflicts between modern modes of living (with their peculiar rationality, technology, social organization, and behaviours) and traditional ways of life.

The two development stories described earlier – asparagus cultivation in Peru and oil extraction in Ecuador – contain each of these four areas. Should the goal of employment creation be pursued or that of environmental sustainability? Can these two goals be reconciled? Does the government have legitimate authority to control the territory and declare ownership of

What is development ethics

core questions

sub–soil resources? Should some communities be allowed to continue their economic practices, such as communal land tenure, even if this contradicts other practices such as legal regime of individual property rights? Which legal system should prevail?

The current dispute surrounding the building of a hydroelectric dam on the land of indigenous communities in Panama constitutes yet another story of how questions about the nature of the good life, how to redistribute resources, who has legitimate authority and how to relate to nature cannot be avoided in development planning and policy.

The establishment of international markets for carbon offsets, such as the Clean Development Mechanism (CDM), is facilitating investment in so-called clean technologies in countries other than the ones in which carbon offsets are bought. Panama is one of the many countries benefiting from this new global scheme aimed at tackling climate change. The Panamanian government has plans to build a series of hydroelectric dams to generate renewable energy. But the dam projects are situated on land inhabited by indigenous communities.[16] They have been battling with the Panamanian state for decades about having their land recognized as a semi-autonomous territory on which they could exercise their self-determination rights as peoples with their specific ways of life. In the case of the Naso people who live near the Changuinola river, this recognition was in its final stage of negotiations when the government stepped back and approved instead the building of a large dam on the river (Finley-Brook and Thomas 2011). The dam will submerge Naso land, displace their communities, undermine the biodiversity of the region and contaminate the river. The Naso are appealing to the Inter-American Court of Human Rights and have blocked roads as a peaceful protest against the government decision.[17]

The companies contracted to build and administer the dam are dividing the indigenous communities by offering some social services and other presents to gain their approval. There are even reports of the government and companies engineering electricity cuts in Panamanian cities to manipulate public opinion and make people believe that more electricity generation capacity is badly needed (Finley-Brook and Thomas 2011). The government rhetoric is that a few thousand people – indigenous peoples and their supporters – are preventing the 'development' of the whole country, a rhetoric echoed in other Latin American countries.[18]

The Panamanian story reflects the four areas of development ethics highlighted by Goulet. First, there is a debate about goals. For most Nasos, the goal they want to pursue is to continue living on their land in harmony with the natural environment. For the Panamanian government, the goal they want to pursue is to generate growth in economic output based on renewable energy sources. Second, there is a debate about power and who has authority. The Naso people do not recognize the legitimacy of the authority of the Panamanian government over their territory. They have their own customary forms of governance, separate from the country's formal political system. There is also contestation of authority within the Naso community. The government and companies negotiated the dam contract with the Naso king, which most Naso people did not recognize as having legitimate authority over them. The Naso elected another leader whose authority the government did not recognize. Third, there is debate about natural resources and how to use them. The Naso people consider the land as their mother and the river as their grandmother. If their land and river are taken away, their lives are taken away too. Finally, there is debate about how people should live, whether living off fishing and farming in communally owned land or living off waged labour in a regime of individual property rights. Are all ways of life equal and compatible with each other?

Despite their contemporary relevance, Goulet's writings have remained sidelined in the academic community. One reason for this neglect is that they were deeply rooted in the practice of development planning and implementation of development projects and did not engage much with academic theorizing – Goulet considered academic philosophy too disconnected from people's lives (Gasper 2008). The other reason is that economics, with its limited, sometimes non-existent concern for normative questions, continued to be the most powerful discipline of development studies.[19] It is not until Amartya Sen reconnected economics with philosophy in his works in social choice and welfare economics that ethics re-entered economics. *relates this issue to Amartya Sen*

Ethics and economics

In a short book entitled *Ethics and Economics*, Sen contrasts what he calls the engineering approach to economics to the ethical approach. The former, he writes,

> is characterized by being concerned with primarily logistic issues rather than with ultimate ends and such questions as what may foster 'the good of man' or 'how should one live?'. The ends are taken as fairly straightforwardly given, and the object of the exercise is to find the appropriate means to serve them.
>
> *(Sen 1987: 3–4)*

Sen's view

Sen argues that the choice of appropriate means cannot be separated from a discussion of the ends they serve. What is the purpose of increasing economic output? What is the purpose of price and market liberalization? Are trade liberalization measures always appropriate? Deliberation about which ends should be pursued, and which means are most appropriate for these ends, characterizes the ethical approach to economics, Sen (1995: 16) compares the failure to deliberate about ends to 'a decision expert whose response to seeing a man engaged in slicing his toes with a blunt knife is to rush to advise him that he should use a sharper knife to better serve his evident objective'.

What Sen calls the engineering approach to economics rests itself upon a certain normative framework: utilitarianism. According to Sen (1999: 58–9), utilitarianism makes three claims: all choices must be judged by their consequences; judgements of state of affairs are restricted to the utility space (with income often used as a proxy for utility); and the goodness, or rightness, of one's action is the sum of all the utilities generated by it.

In the above development stories from Peru, Ecuador and Panama, one can see how the utilitarian framework has underpinned policy decision-making. In the Ica valley, the Peruvian government was concerned with the aim of maximizing the output of the national economy. The decisions that were judged the best were those that most increased economic output. Opening up agriculture to foreign investment and giving special incentives to export-oriented crops were judged as the best means to achieve this single objective. Agro-businesses, too, were concerned with the aim of maximizing their economic output and profits. In Ecuador, the government and mining companies were also guided by the concern of maximizing economic output, and extracting natural resources was judged as the best means of doing so. In Panama, it was the concern for increasing economic output, through the means of electricity generation, which led to the decision to build a hydroelectric dam on Naso land.

It could be argued, however, that the increase in economic output was an intermediate end to achieve other ends. For the Ecuadorian government, the cash generated by the extractive industry was used to pay for health services, schools and infrastructure. In the Ica valley, the increase in economic output led to significant employment creation. In Panama, the greater economic output facilitated by increased electricity capacity was promised to generate government revenues to be invested in better health and education.

But the reality turned more complex. In the Ica valley, the information that asparagus cultivation was water intensive and that the valley was too arid for the crop, was not taken into account in the decision to transform the structure of the economy of the region from small- and medium-scale farming to export-oriented large-scale agriculture. There has been a failure to include in the decision-making process information about the consequences of one's actions on the environment. If another normative framework had guided policy, one which took all relevant factors into consideration and did not assess consequences against the measure of economic output, the Ica valley would have been in another situation than the dilemma in which it is now. In Ecuador, the policy decision to generate government revenues through natural resource extraction has not taken into account the views of the people who are affected by these extractive activities. There have been, however, attempts at introducing another normative framework in policy, one which includes information about the environment and the opportunities indigenous peoples have to maintain their own distinctive cultural, economic, political and social practices.

What Sen's works in ethics and economics have done is to uncover the ethical or normative foundations of economic decisions. Policy decision-making is not a technical enterprise to find the best means to maximize the single objective of maximizing economic output. Even such enterprise relies on a certain normative framework. In Peru, the utilitarian framework has led to a situation of water depletion. In Ecuador and Panama, it has led to social conflict and environmental destruction. What could replace the utilitarian framework?

To the claims made by utilitarianism, Sen has advocated a broad consequentialism (Sen 2000), which broadens the evaluation space of states of affairs to include other information, such as that about human rights or the environment. He has proposed that opportunities people have to live the kind of lives they have reason to value, and not utility levels, best represent a person's wellbeing. He has considered each person as an end, for it is the wellbeing of each individual human being that matters and not the average sum of a population. The next two chapters describe this new normative or ethical framework for policy decision-making. It has been called, for want of a better word, 'the capability approach'.

Notes

1 The section draws on a report entitled 'Drop by drop: Understanding the impacts of the UK's water footprint through a case study of Peruvian asparagus', published in 2010 by Progressio in association with the Centro Peruano de Estudios Sociales and Water Witness International. The full report can be accessed at http://www.progressio.org.uk/sites/default/files/Drop-by-drop_Progressio_Sept-2010.pdf.

2 Some informants spoke of a daily salary increase from US$1 to US$10 in 15 years. Other informants, however, reported that the employment failed to meet the

decent work standards set by the International Labour Office and that 70 per cent of the economically active population of the region worked on temporary contracts ('Drop by drop', pp. 18–19).

3 'Drop by drop', p. 64. A farm labourer receives approximately two and a half pence for a kilo of asparagus harvested, but the same kilo sells for £9.10 in British supermarkets ('Drop by drop', p. 80).

4 Approximately 150 out of the 800 wells in use are estimated to be illegal, and only one of the five drilling companies has been legally licensed to dig ('Drop by drop', p. 69).

5 There were other areas where asparagus could have been cultivated (and which had more water) but mainly because of cheap desert land, the agro-export boom concentrated in the Ica valley ('Drop by drop', p. 68).

6 For a history of development, see Chari and Corbridge (2008), Cowen and Shenton (1996), Escobar (1995), Hettne (2009), Rist (2009) and Sachs (1992). For a discussion on the meaning of development, see Sen (1988) and the seminal paper by Dudley Seers in 1969 at http://www.ids.ac.uk/files/dmfile/themeaning ofdevelopment.pdf.

7 See the 2011 Annual Report by the Revenue Watch Institute on the extractive industry in Latin America at http://www.revenuewatch.org/sites/default/files/Reporte%20RWI_0.pdf.

8 The 2007 Declaration on the Rights of Indigenous Peoples define indigenous peoples as groups who have distinct economic, social, legal and cultural practices from the nation-states in which they live and who seek to be collectively recognized as such. See http://www.un.org/esa/socdev/unpfii/documents/DRIPS_en.pdf.

9 Correa announced on 15 August 2013 that the ITT initiative was dead and has allowed oil companies to drill under the ITT field, placing the blame on industrialized countries' lack of environmental commitment.

10 This will be discussed further in Chapter 3.

11 See http://www.senplades.gob.ec/web/senplades-portal/plan-nacional-para-el-buen-vivir-2009-2013.

12 According to the Revenue Watch Institute (see note 7), Ecuador increased its oil production in 2011 from 500 to 600 barrels a day.

13 According to an Amnesty International report of February 2012, the human rights abuses include criminalization of association of indigenous and environmental groups, searching houses of activists without authorization and detention without charge. See http://movimientos.org/imagen/amnistía%20ecuador.pdf.

14 The picture can be seen on the ECUARUNARI website portal: http://ecuarunari.org/portal.

15 For an assessment of Goulet's work, see Gasper (2008). For a discussion of development ethics, see Gasper (2004, 2012) and Goulet (2006). For a collection of the main publications in the subject, see Gasper and St Clair (2010).

16 See the videos 'Panama: Village of the Damned' by Al-Jazeera at http://interamericana.co.uk/2012/04/al-jazeera-documentary-village-of-the-damned, and 'Message to the world of the Naso indigenous people of Panama' at http://vimeo.com/37544203. For a discussion of the ethical questions that arise from displacement by development, see Penz et al. (2011).

17 According to the documentary made by Al-Jazeera (see note 16), the police dispersed the demonstration by shooting, resulting in some deaths and wounded, including children.

18 The discourse by ex-Peruvian President Alan Garcia on the 'dog in the manger' syndrome has probably been the one most publicized. See http://www. peruviantimes.com/30/president-alan-garcias-policy-doctrinethe-dog-in-the-manger-syndrome/2860.
19 I thank Des Gasper for this argument.

2

LIVING WELL

Wellbeing and agency

Words and grammar of the capability approach

[handwritten margin note: the definition of the capabilities approach]

This book argues that the capability approach is a normative language, which provides the most encompassing framework available to date to judge situations and inform social and political action so as to enable people to live well in a shared natural environment. This chapter and the next will present some of the tools that this normative language offers and how they can help answer, or at least give some outline of answers to, the ethical questions raised by the stories narrated in the previous chapter.

The gist of the capability approach was briefly described in the introduction. This chapter explains, and scrutinizes more deeply, the keywords of this new normative language, which appeared in the social sciences and humanities in the 1980s. Its defining words are few. They have been laid out most comprehensively in Sen's Dewey Lectures, entitled 'Wellbeing, Agency and Freedom' given in 1984 at Columbia University, and published in 1985 in the *Journal of Philosophy*.

The opening sentence of the Dewey Lectures contains the whole essence of this new normative language that Sen is constructing: 'The main aim of the lectures is to explore a moral approach that sees persons from two different perspectives: *wellbeing* and *agency*' (Sen 1985: 169). Sen does not yet talk of a capability approach, but of an approach to morality, the domain of what should be done, which conceives of persons as functioning beings and as agents. Any moral judgement, whether at the individual or policy level, is to be based on these two perspectives, wellbeing and agency. The opening

[handwritten margin note: Sen]

paragraph of the Dewey Lectures concludes by saying that 'each aspect [wellbeing and agency] also yields a corresponding notion of freedom' (Sen 1985: 169). In later writings, Sen (2002: 10) talks of the opportunity and process aspects of freedom:

> Freedom can be valued for the substantive opportunity it gives to the pursuit of our objective and goals. In assessing opportunities, attention has to be paid to the actual ability of a person to achieve those things that she has reason to value. The focus is not directly on what the processes involved happen to be, but on what the real opportunities of achievement are for the persons involved. This 'opportunity aspect' of freedom can be contrasted with another perspective that focuses in particular on the freedom involved in the process itself . . . This is the 'process aspect' of freedom.

normative - ideal type

Thus, Sen offers a moral approach for judging situations from the perspective of freedom, but the view of freedom he proposes is inescapably connected to the twin concepts of wellbeing (opportunity aspect of freedom) and agency (process aspect of freedom). It is, however, not a view of freedom to do or be whatever one wishes at the whim of one's mood – we shall return later to the various misinterpretations of the capability approach and its conception of freedom. Applied to international development, this moral approach conceives development as a process of emancipation or liberation towards greater freedom, that is, towards greater wellbeing and agency. Sen would later summarize this in a book entitled *Development as Freedom* (1999).

In his Dewey Lectures, Sen distinguishes wellbeing from being well-off. The latter is concerned with opulence, with how much a person has, the former with how a person functions, what he or she succeeds in being or doing:

well-off

> The primary feature of well-being can be seen in terms of how a person can 'function'. I shall refer to various doings and beings that come into this assessment as *functionings*. These could be activities (like eating or reading or seeing), or states of existence or being, e.g., being well nourished, being free from malaria, not being ashamed by the poverty of one's clothing or shoes.
>
> (Sen 1985: 197–8)

wellbeing v. well-off

The moral approach which Sen presents is one in which the central moral question is, 'What kind of a life is she [a person] leading? What does she succeed in doing and in being?' (Sen 1985: 195). Sen does not give any indication as to what these 'beings' and 'doings' might be beyond the ones given above.[1] He prefers to use the expression 'to do or be what they have reason to value', without committing himself to specific activities or states of existence people might have reason to value. As he writes, the 'functioning approach is intrinsically information-pluralist' (Sen 1985: 200). A person functions in many aspects and there are many activities she can do and many states she can be. The functionings that people in a fishing community in Greenland have reason to value as part of their human living may be quite different from those of a pastoralist community in Namibia.

To this functioning moral approach, Sen adds another layer and extends it to a person's capability to function:

> The information pluralism of the functioning approach to wellbeing has to be further extended if we shift attention from the person's actual functionings to his or her *capability* to function. A person's *capability set* can be defined as the set of functioning vectors [a functioning vector being the set of functionings a person actually achieves] within his or her reach.
>
> *(Sen 1985: 200–1)*

definition

Sen shifts his moral approach from a functioning to a capability approach so that one can include another type of information in moral evaluation: positive freedom or 'the freedom "to do this" or "to be that" that a person has' (Sen 1985: 201). When one compares two states of affairs and judges whether one is better than another, the capability approach allows for 'comparison of actual opportunities that different persons have' (Sen 1985: 201), and not simply for comparison of actual activities or states of existence, as does the functioning approach.

To illustrate the distinction between the functioning and capability approaches, let us compare the situation of two able-bodied women who have never travelled more than 20 miles away from their home. Both have a car and a driving license but one person lives in England and the other in the Occupied Palestinian Territories. Both are showing the same level of functioning, in this case low mobility but they have very different sets of opportunities. The English woman could travel further away but chooses to spend her life in her immediate surroundings. In contrast, the Palestinian woman does not have any opportunity to travel further than what the checkpoints and Separation Wall allow her to. She has very little freedom to move, in contrast to the English woman. To account for respect for people and the type of life they have reason to value – some may have reason to value a life with low mobility, others a life with high mobility – the capability approach focuses on the opportunities (in this case opportunity to move around) rather than actual outcomes (moving around).

In addition to wellbeing understood in terms of functionings and capabilities, the normative language of the capability approach contains another keyword: agency. Agency and wellbeing are connected but do not always go in the same direction. Agency is the 'pursuit of whatever goals or values he or she regards as important' (Sen 1985: 203). A peasant in the Amazon who resists illegal logging and campaigns to protect the forest may risk his or her own life. Despite the obvious loss of wellbeing, that person exercises agency. In Sen's moral approach, information about agency, and not only wellbeing, has to be included in moral judgements. Sen justifies the inclusion of agency in the informational basis of moral judgement on the ground of recognition of responsibility. Persons are not only functioning, that is, doing certain activities or achieving certain states of existence like moving or being healthy, but they are also responsible: 'The importance of the agency aspect, in general, relates to the view of persons as responsible agents' (Sen 1985: 204).

The moral approach which Sen presents does not say whether one type of information – functioning, capability or agency – is more important than another. Their importance varies according to context:

> The wellbeing aspect may be particularly important in some specific contexts, e.g., in making public provision for social security, or in planning for the fulfilment of basic needs . . . On the other hand, in many issues of personal morality, the agency aspect, and one's responsibility to others may be central. The wellbeing aspect and the agency aspect both demand attention, but they do so in different ways, and with varying relevance to different problems.
>
> *(Sen 1985: 208)*

Agency could therefore be compared to the grammar of the language. It is not only a word but also a verb. People are responsible to decide in each context whether considerations of agency or wellbeing matter more, and if wellbeing matters more, whether considerations of capabilities or function-ings matter more, and if considerations of functionings matter more, which functionings to use as the informational basis of moral judgements. Sen leaves it up to public reasoning processes within each social setting to decide on these matters (Sen 1992, 2004a).

Going back to the situation of the Occupied Palestinian Territories and judging it on the basis of the moral approach that Sen presents, one question to ask would be: is agency, in this case pursuing the goal of self-determination, more important than wellbeing considerations? Many organizations in Palestine are caught up in this dilemma of having to choose wellbeing over agency. An international organization has seen its social projects with local Palestinian communities repeatedly destroyed by the occupying power. Yet, if it questions the Occupation and denounces its illegitimacy and violation of international law, it knows that it will be thrown out of the country immediately and will no longer be able to conduct its activities, leaving the population without key social services which maintain their health and other key human functionings.[2] If considerations for wellbeing are chosen over agency considerations, the question arises whether to give more weight to capabilities or functionings (should one give greater importance to the opportunities people have to move rather than mobility itself?), and which capabilities or which functionings are more important (should the capability to move be given greater priority than the capability to be healthy?). When capabilities interact, such as when the opportunity to reach a hospital or the opportunity to go to school depends on the opportunity to circulate freely on roads, then one should give priority to the capability which influences all of the others the most.[3]

Similar questions arise when judging with the normative language of the capability approach the situation of the Naso people in Panama described in the previous chapter. Should wellbeing considerations matter more than agency? If so, then relocating the Naso people in another environment in which they are able to function in the same way as they were along the Changuinola river, would protect their wellbeing. But it seemed that for the Naso people, considerations of agency mattered more. The goal they valued pursuing was not only functioning as human beings, but functioning as Naso people in that specific territory. Living along another river, in another forest and cultivating another land would strip them of their identity as Naso people, something they valued more than their own wellbeing – some people risked being wounded or even killed in the pursuit of that goal. Should wellbeing considerations have mattered more, the question of giving priority to which capabilities or which functionings would have had to be asked. Should the Naso be resettled, should the resettlement scheme focus on housing and employment opportunities? Should the Naso children attend the same school as other Panamanian children or should they receive a special education which teaches them special skills that children living in Panama City do not need?

The moral approach that Sen presents does not give answers to these questions, and it is even less engaged in the issues of power of configuration which deeply affects which questions are asked and how they are answered. Who decides that wellbeing concerns are more important than agency concerns? Who decides that freedom of movement is not the priority of development efforts in the Occupied Palestinian Territories? Who decides that all Panamanian children should receive the same education independently of their place of living? This book argues that it is right for the capability approach not to answer these questions, and that the critique that it does not sufficiently engage with power and inequality is misplaced.[4] As a normative language, it is not the task of the capability approach as such to answer these questions, just as it is not the task of the English language to tell us how to grow vegetables or how to fix a broken bike. The English language enables us to describe plant physiology or bike mechanics, and so does the capability approach in the moral arena. It offers us a framework to describe a situation from a normative perspective so that people can make choices and act in that situation, but it is not prescriptive about how to act and transform that situation, as shall later be discussed in greater detail.

Thus, the normative perspective that the capability approach offers is that of freedom in its wellbeing and agency aspects, that is, its opportunity or process aspects. But the process aspect of freedom lies also at the core of its opportunity aspect, for wellbeing depends not only on what a person does or is, but on *how* she has achieved that functioning, whether she was actively involved in the process of achieving that functioning or not.[5] Being tube-fed or eating cooked food, eating a ready meal on one's own or eating a home-cooked meal with friends may lead to the same functioning, 'being adequately nourished', but the wellbeing one derives from each is different precisely because the process involved is different. Whether wellbeing is foremost a matter of functioning or agency, the capability approach is open to both characterizations:

> If the wellbeing that a person gets from what she *does* is dependent on *how* she came to do it (in particular, whether she chose that functioning herself), then her well-being depends not just on *x*, but on the choice of *x* from the set *S*. . . . The crucial question here, in the context of wellbeing, is whether freedom to choose is valued only instrumentally, or is also important in itself. The capability approach is broad enough to permit both the rival − but interrelated − characterizations of wellbeing, and can be used in either way.
>
> *(Sen 1992: 150)*

In their work on disadvantage from a capability perspective, Wolff and De-Shalit (2007: 74) argue that the idea of capability is best conceived as freedom to sustain functioning or 'genuine opportunity for secure functioning'. Two people may work and earn a similar wage but one has a permanent contract and the other a one-year renewable contract. They both have the same level of functioning (being employed) and similar opportunities for employment, but one has an opportunity for secure functioning, the other does not. Moreover, functionings are observable, capabilities are often not. How do we know whether the observed lack of functioning is the result of lack of opportunities or personal free choice? Wolff and De-Shalit (2013) argue that it is not so much freedom of choice which matters (whether for example to be healthy or not) but freedom to reach a valuable functioning in one's own way (Sen's process aspect of freedom).

Freedom is an ambiguous concept, and the capability approach, as a moral approach which sees persons from the perspective of freedom, is therefore also ambiguous. As Sen (1993: 33) puts it:

> Insofar as there are genuine ambiguities in the concept of freedom, that should be reflected in corresponding ambiguities in the characterization of capability. This relates to a methodological point . . . that if an underlying idea has an essential ambiguity, a precise formulation of that idea must try to *capture* that ambiguity rather than hide or eliminate it.

This ambiguity has led to quite a few misinterpretations of the idea of freedom as understood by the capability approach.

To make the rather complex concept of capability accessible to a wide non-academic audience, the *Human Development Reports* have translated capability as 'choice'. The 'development as capability expansion' of Sen (1989) has become development as 'a process of enlarging people's choices' (UNDP 1990: 1). This has been a somewhat unfortunate translation as it may confuse the opportunity aspect of wellbeing with consumer choices. Development as capability expansion is not about greater choice of brands or greater choice of health-care providers, but about expanding the opportunities people have to function. Sometimes an increase in 'choices' in the latter sense, such as the choice between a public and private health system, may lead to a decrease in people's opportunities to function. The introduction of a dual health system may lead to a disinvestment in public health services and exclude some people from accessing health care. Another confusion which has been made is that of lapsing 'development as freedom' with market freedom. Greater freedom to buy and exchange goods in markets can sometimes increase people's opportunities to be or do what they have reason to value but sometimes, greater market regulation better achieves that objective. If there had been greater regulation of financial markets, the global financial crisis which has affected many people's capabilities to be employed, adequately sheltered or fed, especially those already in a disadvantaged economic and social situation, could have been avoided.

Sen presented his moral approach as an alternative to the moral approach widespread in the discipline of economics to judge a social reality. Instead of using utility as information for moral judgement, one is to use information about wellbeing and agency. Let us now turn to some of the ways in which the language has been used to judge, from a moral perspective, various situations.

A normative language to assess situations

One of the most publicized uses of the capability approach to assess situations differently from the utilitarian moral approach has been the publication of the *Human Development Reports*. The real wealth of a nation is not how much it produces or consumes but how well people live in that nation. The capability approach does not deny the importance of resources and income for determining how well people are able to function as human beings, but these are only means to ends. As far as moral judgement is concerned, one needs to focus on the ends and whether the means further the ends, whether people have opportunities to function well and exercise agency with the resources or income they have. In the jargon of the capability approach this is called 'conversion factors', or the factors which allow, or do not allow, people to convert the resources and income they have into functionings and capabilities.

A family may have considerable assets but the daughters may not be able to function well in the area of knowledge and education because of social norms which maintain that a woman's place is at home and that girls do not need to be educated. A family may have a car but may be unable to travel because of a restriction on freedom of movement. To achieve the same functioning of being healthy, a family will need to earn more income than another if it lives in a country without free universal healthcare. To achieve the same functioning of being sheltered and keeping warm, one will need a different amount of resources if one lives in the Caribbean or Southern Chile. As has been shown extensively in the *Human Development Reports*, there is no straightforward positive link between a country's material wealth and how well its people are able to live. Income distribution, social expenditures and levels of education, especially female education, also matter (Ranis and Stewart 2012).

In what follows, two recent applications of the capability approach as a normative language to assess situations are discussed. These applications have been selected to highlight the different interpretations that users of the language make in the light of their context of analysis and their audience. As the next section will show, these two applications contain in a nutshell the variety of interpretations which are found in the secondary literature on the capability approach. The first application is that of the Multidimensional Poverty Index, the second is that of the National Human Development Report of the Dominican Republic.

The Multidimensional Poverty Index

For decades, international poverty measures have consisted in counting the number of people living below the poverty line – usually set at the amount of money a family needs for meeting some minimal food and shelter requirements. These measures have been based on the language of neo-classical economics and its conception of wellbeing in terms of utility, with income or consumption as proxies for measuring utility. In contrast, the Multidimensional Poverty Index (MPI), designed by the Oxford Poverty and Human Development Initiative (OPHI), measures poverty with the language of the capability approach and its understanding of wellbeing in terms of how well people are able to function as human beings, in terms of what they have reason to value being or doing. It singles out three dimensions of wellbeing and is measured by ten indicators which have been chosen for international comparison purposes on the basis of existing data availability: health (nutrition, child mortality), education (years of schooling, school attendance) and living standards (cooking fuel, sanitation, electricity, floor and assets). A person is poor if he or she is deprived in at least one dimension or one-third of the weighted indicators. The MPI looks at how deprived each person is. It 'assesses the nature and intensity of poverty at the individual level'.[6]

The differences between income and multidimensional poverty are quite striking in some cases. In 2010, researchers at OPHI estimated that 53.7 per cent of the Indian population was multi-dimensionally poor. This compares to the 37.2 per cent of the population below the national poverty line according to data from the Indian government.[7] The OPHI team has drafted dozens of country briefings which show the differences between measuring poverty in terms of income and basic functionings. In Colombia, only 5.4 per cent of the population was multi-dimensionally poor in 2010, that is, not functioning well in at least a third of the above ten indicators, compared to 16 per cent living with less than US$1.25 a day. For 2006 data, Nicaragua had 28 per cent of multi-dimensionally poor people, compared to 15.8 per cent of people living with less than US$1.25 a day (2005 data). In Pakistan, 49.4 per cent of the population was estimated to be multi-dimensionally poor in 2007, compared to 22.6 per cent of income poor in 2006.[8] Thus the normative language one uses to describe a situation matters. The number of people living in poverty increases or decreases according to how poverty is normatively conceived, whether as a lack of income or lack of functionings.

Which normative language one uses to judge situations will also have implications for actions which follow from the judgement. If one uses the neo-classical language and income poverty as the word to describe poverty, the action one will take to change a situation of poverty so that it becomes closer to the normative objective (sufficient income to buy a basket of basic commodities), will typically focus on raising people's incomes and pushing people above the income poverty line. For example, the Indian government pursued market liberalization which led to an unprecedented rate of economic growth, at about 8 per cent average in the last ten years (Drèze and Sen 2011). These policies reduced the number of income poor significantly. According to World Bank estimates, the poverty headcount ratio, calculated at the national poverty line, was 45.3 per cent in 1994. In 2010, only 29.8 per cent of the population was estimated to be poor.[9] In contrast, if one uses the capability approach as a normative language to describe the situation of poverty in India, the action one will take to pursue the normative objective (that people have opportunities to function well as human beings) will typically focus on redistribution and social policies to ensure that people have opportunities to achieve some functionings, such as being healthy and being well nourished. Judged from the perspective of the capability approach, the assessment of India's economic policies is less of a successful story. It is, what Drèze and Sen (2013) have entitled in their book, an 'uncertain glory', as will be discussed at length in Chapter 3.

The Dominican National Human Development Report

Another application of the capability approach has been the *Human Development Reports* at the international, regional and national levels. It is impossible to review here the hundreds of reports produced over the last 20 years. For the purpose of the argument, this section shall focus on one national report, which exemplifies quite a different interpretation from that of the MPI. Instead of providing data on multidimensional poverty, the 2008 *National Human Development Report* published by the UNDP office of the Dominican Republic, entitled 'Human Development: A Question of Power', provides a rich analysis of the configuration of power in the country.[10] It argues that one of the main obstacles which prevents people from having opportunities to be or do what they have reason to value, such as being educated or healthy, is inequality. The report examines how social inequality leads to political inequality and exclusion from political participation, which then furthers social exclusion. As the report says in its prologue:

> In a society like the Dominican one, of large social, economic and institutional inequality, access to opportunities is determined by individual power or the group to which one belongs . . . What is tragic for the country is that, in the long term, inequality in opportunities has not been the consequence of lack of economic resources, but of the bad decisions of those who have held power to decide how to spend these resources.

In this regard, the report gives the example of the building of a new metro line in Santo Domingo as symptomatic of this unequal power distribution. Significant public resources have been invested into this infrastructure project but the new metro line has been built in a low population density area which benefits the middle and upper economic classes. The metro could have been built in a much higher population density area where it would have benefited more people and decongested traffic. Also, the metro project led to the diversion of large public resources, which could have been invested in social infrastructure in poor urban areas where the vast majority of people lacking basic opportunities live.

Given the specific social reality it analyses and the audience it seeks to influence, the National Human Development Report of the Dominican Republic interprets capabilities not only at the individual level but also at a social level. Therefore the report assesses wellbeing not only in terms of individual characteristics, such as the sets of doings and beings of individuals, but also in terms of institutional characteristics which do not belong to any individual in particular. These include the distribution of political power in the country and the nature of political institutions through which people can voice their concerns about lack of opportunities to do or be what they have reason to value, such as lack of opportunities to live a healthy life or be adequately sheltered. For example, the opportunity the daughter of Haitian immigrants has to be healthy depends very much on how the Dominican society as a whole treats Haitian immigrants and their children. This is why the report has attempted to include in its analysis the quality of social relations and political structures, and the extent to which all Dominican citizens are able to participate in them and transform the political reality to ensure a fairer distribution of power.

There are many other applications of the capability approach in the social sciences. One can use it to assess whether the introduction of Information and Communication Technology in a remote rural area increases people's wellbeing and agency. One can use it to assess whether certain pedagogies are better than others from the perspective of students' wellbeing and agency.[11] What is common to these applications is that they each had to *interpret* the language in their own context and construct their own judgements of a situation given the audience they speak to. The audience of the multidimensional poverty index is economists and policymakers who have been using income measures of poverty to design poverty-reduction policy. The audience of the Dominican National Human Development Report is Dominican civil society organizations which are engaged in improving the lives of the marginalized and socially excluded in the Dominican Republic. The next section turns to how the language has been interpreted in different contexts.

Interpreting the language

The basic structure of the normative language of the capability approach has been written in many texts.[12] Like any text, they were written by a particular author, who was situated in a specific reality and speaking to an audience with a specific intention. Sen wrote primarily for neo-classical economists with the intention to demonstrate some problems with neo-classical economics (the use of utility as an approximation of human wellbeing), and for liberal egalitarian philosophers with the intention to demonstrate some problems with Rawls's theory of justice (the use of primary goods as the informational basis of justice).

As a 'discourse fixed by writing' (Ricoeur 1981: 144), a text is there to be read, but to read is always 'to fulfil the text in present speech' (Ricoeur 1981: 144), 'to conjoin a new discourse to the discourse of the text' (Ricoeur 1981: 158). Reading a text is about relating its basic structure to the specific reality of the reader, about translating it to the reader's world. Therefore, like any text, the texts which fix the basic structure of the capability approach are open to interpretation, in the sense that the meaning of the original texts is always to be reconstructed by the reader according to his or her own reality. The work of interpretation is particularly needed as Sen has left the basic structure of the capability approach purposively incomplete and ambiguous. As he acknowledges, it is a general approach 'with various bits to be filled in' (Sen 1993: 48).[13]

This section highlights two main areas of interpretation: its conception of the person and its purpose. The diversity of interpretations need not be seen as a problem but as a strength, for it signals the versatility of the language to adapt itself to different contexts and audiences. Each interpretation need not be seen as mutually exclusive of another but a reflection of the context in which the language is used and spoken. When used by an economist to measure poverty, by a lawyer to stop human rights abuses, by a philosopher to discuss human freedom or by a sociologist to understand social norms, the language will still contain the same keywords of functionings, capabilities and agency, but it will be used to construct different sentences and stories given the purpose of the analysis and its audience.

Conception of the person

As presented above, the capability approach is a moral approach, which conceives of the person as free. This freedom has two perspectives: wellbeing and agency. A person is free when he or she has the opportunity to function (as a human being) and to pursue goals he or she values. This central place of human freedom has led some to interpret the capability approach as firmly situated within the liberal philosophical tradition (Robeyns 2009). According to that interpretation, the capability approach does not presuppose a comprehensive doctrine of the good and, consistent with the basic tenets of liberalism, leaves people free to decide what conception of the human good they want to pursue. In an argument with John Rawls about his concern that capabilities are in essence judgements about what is worthwhile, and implicitly rely on a judgement about the nature of a good human life, Sen (1990: 118) responds that: 'Capability reflects a person's *freedom* to choose between alternative lives (functioning combinations), and its value need not be derived from one particular "comprehensive doctrine" demanding one specific way of living'. This is why Sen does not define which valuable capabilities should enter the evaluation space, and talks of the 'capabilities people have reason to value'. It is up to processes of public reasoning within each society or context to define what is valuable. This is to respect people's freedom to decide for themselves on these matters.

But this interpretation need not be the only one. When Sen wrote the basic texts of the capability approach, his audience was that of political philosophy and most academic arguments in the field evolved around Rawls's *Theory of Justice* (1971). The language can be interpreted differently when taken to another audience. Martha Nussbaum was the first to take the capability approach in another direction by linking valuable capabilities to a particular conception of the human good, thus adopting a teleological conception of the person. Living as a human being has an end, which is to live well. What constitutes human wellbeing, to live well as a human being, is not whatever each individual freely decides for him- or herself. Nussbaum proposed a 'thick vague theory of the good' with her list of central human capabilities (Nussbaum 1992, 1993). Her list contains the following capabilities: to live a life of normal length; to have bodily health; to have bodily integrity; to think and reason (this includes guarantees of freedom of expression); to express emotions; to engage in critical reflection about the planning of one's life; to engage in social interaction and have the social bases of self-respect; to live with concern for the natural environment; to laugh and play; to control one's environment (this includes participation in political choices that govern one's life and work) (Nussbaum 2000: 77–8; 2011: 33–4). The list remains open-ended in the sense that each central human capability can have many specifications given local contexts, and that other central human capabilities can be added (for example, over the years, Nussbaum has added the capability to hold property rights as a central human capability). Sen had no objection to this interpretation, as long as it was not the only one (Sen 1993).[14]

In addition to whether human life has an end, namely the perfection of the human good, there has been a divergence of interpretations about how the capability approach conceives of the human person as an individual or collective body. According to one interpretation, the capability approach is said to be ethically individualist, in the sense that states of affairs should be evaluated only according to their goodness or badness for individuals (Robeyns 2005, 2008). Economic structures, social norms, informal and formal institutions are assessed according to their impact on individual lives. The caste system or family relations do not enter into wellbeing evaluation, only their effects on individual capabilities, such as employment opportunities, morbidity, bodily integrity, malnutrition and educational opportunities. The caste system or family relations as such are not part of the assessment of social arrangements.

One reason for this commitment to ethical individualism is that a focus on groups or institutions may hide forms of oppressions and inequalities within the group (Alkire 2008b). Focusing on the family as a collective unit may hide the fact that, while enabling the flourishing of some members, it may be oppressive to others. How a 'good' family is defined is often the product of power relations with women having no voice (Robeyns 2008). On this interpretation, it is individuals, and the opportunities they have to function, not groups, who are to be the relevant units of moral valuation. This is also the interpretation favoured by Sen, at least in his theoretical writings.[15] He argues that it is sufficient to recognize individual interdependence and interaction, and the ability of individuals to participate in social life. There is no need for the structures which arise from that interdependence to be part of the moral evaluation of states of affairs, or the object of justice:

There is indeed no particular analytical reason why group capabilities must be excluded a priori from the discourse on justice and injustice. The case for not going that way lies in the nature of the reasoning that would be involved. . . . Ultimately, it is individual evaluation on which we would have to draw, while recognizing the profound interdependence of the valuation of individuals who interact with each other. . . . In valuing a person's ability to take part in the life of society, there is an implicit valuation of the life of the society itself, and that is an important enough aspect of the capability perspective.

(Sen 2009: 246)

There is, however, another interpretation in the capability literature. Because persons interact and are in relation with each other, they create something which is beyond them and which therefore should be part of any normative language which aims at articulating the goodness or badness of social arrangements. Because relations are constitutive of human life, these relations acquire an existence beyond the control of any individual life (Deneulin 2008, Evans 2002, Ibrahim 2013). This does not mean that they are immune to change, but no individual as such has control over them. For example, the economic structure may be the result of individual interactions, of how individuals produce and consume goods, but it also profoundly shapes the opportunities people have to live well. A society structured by an unregulated economic system which prioritizes the maximization of short-term profits over considerations for human wellbeing may create fewer opportunities for valuable functionings than one structured by an economic system which puts the wellbeing of the workers above the maximization of profits. A society structured by a political system based on racial superiority of a few creates fewer opportunities for valuable functionings than one structured by a political system which sees everyone as having equal political, social and economic opportunities.

According to this interpretation, collecting information about individual wellbeing only, including the ability of individuals to participate in society, omits a very important aspect of human life, namely that human life is embedded in a complex web of structural relations which do not belong to any individual as such. The quality of these structural relations matters in judging the goodness or badness of social arrangements. Taking the case of climate change, it will not be sufficient to analyse the consequences of climate change for individual capabilities, one will also need to include information about the quality of relationships between people and their environment, whether characterized by respect or by domination.[16]

In relation to this area of interpretation, there have also been recent debates regarding the anthropocentrism of the approach, whether the environment, and the functioning of ecosystems, should be considered in the evaluation of states of affairs only to the extent in which it affects human wellbeing or also for its intrinsic value independently of human life. Nussbaum has included the capability 'to live with concern for and in relation to animals, plants and the natural environment' (2000: 80), among her central human capabilities, but this is still instrumental to human flourishing. As for Sen, he argues that even if preserving the spotted owl is of no use as such to human wellbeing, if people have come to the conclusion, through processes of public reasoning which stand public scrutiny, that preserving the spotted owl is a valuable thing to do, then this should be respected (Sen 2004b). In his latest book with Jean Drèze, he sees the 'the expansion of freedom', 'the removal of poverty' and 'paying attention to ecology' as 'integral parts of a unified concern' (Drèze and Sen 2013: 43). Thus the language can accommodate different interpretations. It can be interpreted as an anthropocentric evaluation framework, but it also allows for the functioning of ecosystems and biodiversity to be in included as valuable functionings in their own right in the evaluation of states of affairs.

Purpose of the language

The second major area of divergence of interpretations relates to the purpose of the language. In a review article, Alkire (2005: 122) interprets the capability approach as a 'proposition' that 'social arrangements should be evaluated according to the extent of freedom people have to promote or achieve functionings they value'. It provides an alternative informational basis for moral judgements to that of utility but falls short of being prescriptive about what type of information to include. It only advocates that the evaluation of social arrangements be in capability space, which can include a whole range of functionings and capabilities at both the individual and collective or structural level. Alkire (2008b) refers to the 'narrow' interpretation of the capability approach when used for evaluation, and 'broad' or 'prospective' interpretation when used for informing social action.

In another review article, Robeyns (2005: 96) talks of the capability approach as being 'primarily and mainly a framework for thought', a 'broad normative framework for the evaluation and assessment of individual well-being and social arrangements' (2005: 94). She argues that poverty, inequality and social exclusion are not social phenomena that the capability approach seeks to explain. It only aims at conceptualizing them in the light of individual freedom, and would need to be accompanied by explanatory theories. Taking the case of climate change, the capability approach provides a language to assess the situation of some farming community whose livelihoods are affected by changing climate patterns. Instead of judging their situation from the perspective of income losses caused by failed crops, it judges the situation in terms of opportunities people have to do or be what they have reason to value. But according to this interpretation, it is not the task of the capability approach to explain why a specific farming community is experiencing wellbeing losses and even less what the root causes of climate change are.

Another interpretation of the capability approach holds that the purpose of the language is not limited to judging situations. By shedding a specific light on a reality, it also provides tools for social action to transform that reality. In other words, the capability approach is not only a framework for evaluating social arrangements or analysing social phenomena, it is also a partial theory of justice, as the next chapter will explore in detail.

From the above discussion, it becomes clear that the capability approach is not a set of dogmas to apply to the reality of people's lives. This section has highlighted two major, equally valid, areas of interpretation, depending on the context in which the language is being used. It has also highlighted that some interpretations are to be rejected, such as reading the capability approach as another name for human resources and a justification for investment in health and education for the sake of economic growth, or reducing capabilities to mere choices instead of opportunities for human flourishing. As Ricoeur underlined in his discussion of hermeneutics, not all interpretations are equal, some will need to be validated and sometimes no agreement can be found about their validity. As he puts it:

> If it is true that there is always more than one way of construing a text, it is not true that all interpretations are equal. . . . The text is a limited field of possible constructions. The logic of validation allows us to move between the two limits of dogmatism and scepticism. It is always possible to argue against an interpretation, to confront interpretations, to arbitrate between them and to seek for an agreement, even if this agreement remains beyond our reach.
>
> *(Ricoeur 1981: 213)*

The MPI illustrates the tension between the two interpretations that this chapter highlights. On the one hand, the MPI sits clearly within the interpretation of the capability approach as an evaluation framework for social arrangements, and not as a partial theory of justice. The MPI is not designed to understand the causes of poverty and to propose a programme of action to remedy it. It simply evaluates states of affairs. It also sits on the interpretation of the capability approach as embracing ethical individualism, for it tries to capture poverty at the individual level. On the other hand, the MPI opens itself up to other interpretations. By offering a vivid description of the nature and intensity of deprivation, it does point to policy failures, such as the failure to provide adequate nutrition and sanitation. It thus goes beyond being an evaluation tool to informing social and political action. Neither does the MPI's strong individual focus rule out the assessment of social arrangements at a more structural level. The OPHI 2011 MPI Policy Brief describes the life of Adil in West Bengal beyond the three dimensions and ten indicators which constitute the MPI.[17] His employment opportunities depend on personal and social relations which are often exploitative. The securing of basic functionings, such as being nourished and being sheltered, is immersed in a complex set of patron–client relationships which give him some functionings but also deprive him of agency. The evaluation space of social arrangements could be broadened to include data on the quality of structural relations, such as the nature and intensity of clientelism, or the nature and intensity of political inequality in democratic institutions. In that respect Drèze and Sen (2013) provide an in-depth analysis of the nature of political inequality in India and how it affects the opportunities that hundreds of millions of Indians have to achieve a basic set of valuable functionings in the area of health, nutrition, education and employment.

The capability approach and the wellbeing turn

Since the launch of the *Human Development Reports* in 1990 to shift the assessment of how well countries were doing from what people had to how they were able to live with what they had, there have been many other similar initiatives to shift how the progress of societies has been assessed so far. I conclude this chapter by looking at how the normative language of the capability approach situates itself in relation to other approximations of wellbeing in the social sciences and what can be called the 'wellbeing turn', or some might say the 'happiness turn', in policy at the national and international level.

In 1974, the economist Richard Easterlin conducted an empirical study, correlating countries' GDP per capita with the happiness of the population, as measured by how happy people felt on a scale from 0 to 10. His findings were that people became happier as their country grew richer, but that this reached a platform. After a certain level of income, increases in income did not lead to higher levels of happiness among the population.[18] If higher incomes did not make people happier after a certain level, then why continue to have economic growth as policy goal, he asked.

Since Easterlin's study, research on happiness has grown exponentially and the assumption that higher incomes lead to higher utility levels, as expressed by how happy people felt, has been put under even greater scrutiny.[19] In 2012, the first *World Happiness Report* was published.[20] It takes happiness as (1) the 'ups and downs of daily emotions' and (2) 'an individual's overall evaluation of life' (p. 7). The former understanding of happiness is linked to what gives rise to positive or negative emotions like friendships, especially intimate relations, commute to work or relations with colleagues. The latter is linked to what brings satisfaction with life as a whole like meaningful work, sense of contributing to society, good health, good relationships with people or a peaceful environment. The *World Happiness Report* strongly questions the relationships between economic growth and happiness, and urges that the goal of public policy is to enable people to live happier lives and not make the economy grow. When economic growth leads to unhealthier diet habits, higher levels of obesity, higher levels of stress, higher employment insecurity, higher levels of family breakdowns or when it destroys the natural environment, keeps billions of people living in crammed housing conditions with poor hygiene and undermining their health, the policy goal of economic growth needs to be reconsidered.

The tiny Kingdom of Bhutan was the first nation to name happiness as a policy goal in the late 1970s. Its Gross National Happiness Index is now an inspiration for other countries. In contrast to the above conception of happiness as emotion or life satisfaction, it conceives of happiness as spanning nine different domains: psychological wellbeing, time use, community vitality, cultural diversity, ecological resilience, living standard, health, education and good governance. The Index is based on 33 cluster indicators which relate to these domains (Ura *et al.* 2012). It considers happiness more as human fulfilment, as living out one's potential as a human being, than as an emotion or subjective state of satisfaction. It sees life satisfaction as only one dimension of what it means to live a happy and fulfilled life.

The OECD is also working on a composite wellbeing index for its member countries. Its Better Life Index includes ten domains (housing, income, jobs, community, education, environment, civic engagement, life satisfaction, safety, work–life balance) and a series of indicators for each domain. As for the weight assigned to each domain in the overall index, users can choose their own weight and compare countries accordingly.[21]

France had a special commission in 2007 on the 'Measurement of Economic Performance and Social Progress' to design new indicators of wealth to measure not the economy, but how people were doing. The

chosen dimensions comprised material living standards, subjective evalua-
tions of how one was satisfied with one's life, health, education, work,
political voice and governance, social connections and relationships, and
economic security and the environment.[22] The Office of National Statistics
in the UK is currently designing new indicators of national wellbeing to
include information about, among others, life satisfaction, unemployment,
crime, family stability, health, financial security and the environment.[23]

As the above policy initiatives reveal, wellbeing is approximated in both
subjective and objective ways: by asking people how happy they are or how
satisfied they are with their lives (subjective wellbeing), or by observing how
well they fare in certain areas of life such as work, health and security,
independently of what they think about it (objective wellbeing).[24] This
division between objective and subjective wellbeing has, however, been
contested. First, happiness, as a subjective state of how one feels, has an
'objective' neurological dimension. The feeling of happiness is a 'physiological
sensation caused by neuro-chemical response of the dopamine system of brain
to external stimuli' (Phillips 2006: 16). There is therefore a close link between
the subjective state and objective circumstances that generate the chemical
response which causes positive emotions or happiness. These include physical
exercise, work and contribution to society and social interaction, especially at
the intimate level. Second, how well one is satisfied with life depends on the
fulfilment of some psychological needs. According to psychologists Ryan and
Deci (2000), there are basic psychological needs, which, if not fulfilled, lead
to empirical observable harm. These needs are: autonomy (the need to choose
what one is doing, being an agent of one's own life), competence (the need
to feel confident in doing what one is doing) and relatedness (the need to have
human connections that are close and secure).[25]

The capability approach has long been ranked among the 'objective'
categorization of wellbeing. This is due to its critique of utility, or
preferences, as approximations of wellbeing. People can live in objectively
poor circumstances but still report themselves relatively happy. A study
conducted by Biswas-Diener and Diener (2001) among the pavement-
dwellers of Calcutta reported their relatively high levels of life satisfaction.
The authors of the study explained this puzzle by on the one hand, the
phenomenon of 'focusing illusion' whereby one judges another person's
circumstance by focusing on some attributes (material deprivation) and
ignoring others (dense social relations), and on the other to the fact that they
derived life satisfaction from close relationships and living a meaningful life
by showing respect to other people, instead of from material prosperity.
However, one could also attribute this discrepancy between their objective
and subjective wellbeing to adaptation. Because they have always lived in

materially deprived circumstances, they have adapted to their situation and have learned to be satisfied with what they have – relationships – rather than what appears out of reach and what they perceive as unobtainable – a decent standard of living.[26]

While it remains true that the capability approach is about assessing wellbeing from the perspective of 'objective' circumstances of life such as opportunities to be healthy, to be well nourished, to participate in decisions which affect one's life, to move freely and form associations, it also has a 'subjective' dimension. Life satisfaction and positive emotions (happiness) is also a valuable capability, among others.[27] The focus on agency makes the capability approach close to psychological theories, which have underlined the importance of autonomy for how well people were satisfied with their lives. And finally, the 'valuable' capabilities which constitute the 'objective' wellbeing evaluation space are inter-subjective, for they are the results of processes of public reasoning.[28]

In sum, with its inclusion of functionings and capabilities in the evaluation of states of affairs, the capability approach sees human wellbeing in terms of both being and living well. More fundamentally, however, it sees agency, doing something for oneself and for others, contributing to creating or changing one's social, economic, political, cultural and natural environment, as the hallmark of a human life well lived. This is, this book argues, one of the greatest contributions of the normative language of the capability approach to the social sciences. It does not only provide an encompassing framework to conceptualize wellbeing, it also links wellbeing to responsibilities people have towards each other and their wellbeing. In other words, it moves the discussion from wellbeing to justice. Living well and acting justly are inseparable, and the next chapter turns to this topic.

Notes

1 In his 1979 Tanner Lectures, Sen (1980: 218) spoke of 'basic capabilities' such as the 'ability to move about', 'ability to meet one's nutritional requirements, the wherewithal to be clothed and sheltered, the power to participate in the social life of the community'.

2 Oral communication from Palestinian members of staff working in international development organizations in the Occupied Territories.

3 Wolff and De Shalit (2007) talk of these capabilities which influence others as 'fertile' capabilities.

4 For a critique of the capability approach on the ground of its silence regarding the unjust and alienating nature of the capitalist economic system, see Bagchi (2000), Dean (2009) and Feldman (2010).

5 This is why Martha Nussbaum does not follow Sen's wellbeing/agency distinction and captures the idea of agency with the functioning/capability distinction (Nussbaum 2000).

6 See policy brief 'Multidimensional Poverty Index 2011' at www.ophi.org.uk.
7 See 'MPI Country Brief: India' at http://www.ophi.org.uk/wp-content/uploads/India.pdf?cda6c1.
8 See http://www.ophi.org.uk/multidimensional-poverty-index/mpi-country-briefings.
9 See http://data.worldbank.org/country/india.
10 The report is available in Spanish only at http://hdr.undp.org/en/reports/national/latinamericathecaribbean/dominicanrep/NHDR_2008_Dominican Rep.pdf.
11 See Robeyns (2006) for a summary of the practical applications of the capability approach; Oosterlaken and van den Hoven (2012) for how the capability approach can be used in the area of ICT; and Walker (2012) for the use of the capability approach in higher education pedagogies. See also the thematic groups of the Human Development and Capability Association for the various uses of the capability approach (www.hd-ca.org).
12 Among the foundational texts are Sen (1980, 1985, 1992, 1993, 1999).
13 Robeyns (2008: 84) has similarly argued that the capability approach has been the subject of different interpretations according to the scholar's own disciplinary or even religious or ideological lens. She contends that the most truthful interpretation, in the sense of closer to Sen's roots, is the one which understands the capability approach within the background of welfare economics and liberal political philosophy. This book departs from Robeyns's view by arguing that there are other valid interpretations because Sen has purposively left the roots of the approach ambiguous and open-ended.
14 Since the mid-1990s, Nussbaum has changed her position regarding the teleological nature of human life. She no longer considers her list of central human capabilities as a 'thick vague conception of the good' but, following Rawls's political liberalism, as the result of an overlapping consensus between people who hold different comprehensive views of the human good. People need to have access to central human capabilities in order to pursue their own conception of the good. This may include a life which does not make use of certain capabilities, such as political participation. Nussbaum justifies her shift on the ground of respect for people who pursue conceptions of the good with which we disagree (Nussbaum 2000, 2011, 2013).
15 As will be discussed in Chapter 3, in his recent collaborative work with Jean Drèze, there seems to have been a move away from ethical individualism towards structural assessment of societies.
16 See also Alexander (2010) for why the capability approach needs to include a republican understanding of freedom as non-dominating relationships and not simply as individual opportunities.
17 See http://www.ophi.org.uk/wp-content/uploads/OPHI-MPI-Brief-2011.pdf.
18 Easterlin repeated his study 35 years later and reached similar findings (Easterlin *et al.* 2010).
19 It is impossible to summarize here the extent of the vast literature on happiness, but see, among others, Frey (2008), Layard (2005) and Seligman (2011).
20 See http://www.earth.columbia.edu/sitefiles/file/Sachs%20Writing/2012/World%20Happiness%20Report.pdf.
21 See http://www.oecdbetterlifeindex.org.
22 See http://www.stiglitz-sen-fitoussi.fr/en/index.htm.
23 See http://www.ons.gov.uk/ons/guide-method/user-guidance/well-being/index.html.

24 The literature on human wellbeing is vast. See, among others, Gough and McGregor (2007), Phillips (2006), McGillivray (2006) and White (2010).
25 They have named their findings 'self-determination theory'. For a summary of research and application of the theory, see http://www.selfdetermination theory.org.
26 For a discussion of the relation between the capability approach and adaptation, see Clark (2012).
27 See Bruni *et al.* (2008) for a discussion on the capability and happiness literatures.
28 Sen (2009: 122) talks of the 'demands of ethical objectivity' as being closely related to 'the ability to stand up to open public reasoning'.

3

ACTING JUSTLY

Relations and responsibility

A capability view of justice

The previous chapter emphasized that the normative language of the capability approach saw human beings in the particular light of wellbeing and agency, which it conceived in terms of the freedom to do or be what one has reason to value and the freedom to act and do something valuable for oneself and for others. It concluded that, in addition to providing a framework to assess human wellbeing in an encompassing way, including subjective states like life satisfaction, and objective circumstances like bodily health, cognitive attainment and participation in political and social life, the capability approach provided a framework for social transformation so that wellbeing could be enhanced. This chapter continues to focus on the keywords of the normative language and how social actors interpret them in their specific contexts. When moving from wellbeing to justice, from assessing how well people live to how to structure social, political and economic arrangements, this chapter argues that the language contains exactly the same keywords – wellbeing and agency – but links them more closely via the action of reasoning. The opportunities people have to live well (capabilities) are inseparable from what people do, how they act towards each other and their environment. Living well and acting justly go together. This is the argument that this chapter will develop.

From wellbeing to justice

It is with the publication of *The Idea of Justice* (Sen 2009) that the capability approach moved more explicitly from a language with which to speak about the reality of people's wellbeing to a language with which to speak about how that wellbeing can be brought about. The capability approach is no longer a language with which to assess people's wellbeing, it also becomes a language with which to assess how people relate to each other and what types of relations and institutional arrangements, or opportunities to do or be what they have reason to value, best expand their wellbeing. From the question of how to assess equality, the capability approach has moved to the question of how to arrange societies. In other words, it has moved beyond the sphere of wellbeing to the sphere of justice. As the capability approach had to be placed against the background of utilitarian economics – with capabilities replacing the utility space for assessing wellbeing – so it has to be placed against the background of Rawls's theory of justice – with capabilities replacing primary goods as the informational basis of social justice and replacing a procedural account of justice with a comparative account.

Rawls framed his theory of justice on the basis of respect for the diversity of views about what constitutes a good life. Is the ascetic life of a Buddhist monk better than the high-spending life of a business entrepreneur? Is the life of a housewife or househusband better than the life of a corporate lawyer? Rawls's argument is that the diversity of views about what constitutes good living is a fact of modern democratic life and that one cannot, and should not, arbitrate between different conceptions of the good. At least, this is not a requirement for living peacefully as citizens of a democratic state. What is required, Rawls argues, is that societies be arranged by some structuring principles so that all can live well, in whatever way they understand it, peacefully alongside each other. One such principle is that each individual be endowed with a set of primary goods, which are basic fundamental liberties (such as freedom of speech, association and movement), social bases of self-respect and a certain amount of income and resources (Rawls 1993: 194). A society in which some people do not have freedom of movement because of their gender is not a just society, neither is a society in which those who critique the president or main ruling party are intimidated or jailed.

Sen's first critique of Rawls is that, given human diversity, different people will need different amounts of primary goods in order to pursue the same conception of the good (Sen 1990). A disabled person will need a different amount of resources from that required by an able-bodied person to live a life which includes mobility. A severely dyslexic person will need a different amount of resources to live a life which includes writing.[1] But Sen nonetheless stays within the Rawlsian framework when it comes to making judgements about the good life as a requirement of justice. For Sen, as for Rawls, we do not need to know what a good human life consists of in order to say something about how society should be arranged. The difference between them is that, for Rawls, what is needed is a set of principles to distribute primary goods in such a way as to enable them to pursue their own conception of the good. For Sen, in contrast, one does not need such distributive principles in order to structure human relations and provide conditions for people to pursue their conception of the good. What is needed, Sen argues, is 'to examine the capabilities that we can actually enjoy' (Sen 1990: 121). This is Sen's second critique of Rawls and a major point of departure between the two accounts of justice.

While Rawls's intellectual exercise is to find out what just social arrangements are, Sen avoids that exercise, for societies will never be structured in such a way as to be fully just. In a paper entitled 'What do we want from a theory of justice?', Sen (2006) describes the foundations of his *Idea of Justice* and argues that having a comparative framework to assess situations is sufficient to address injustices in the world. Instead of concentrating on how institutions are to be structured, which principles they need to respect, a 'comparative approach would concentrate instead on ranking alternative social arrangements' (Sen 2006: 216). He proposes that the capability approach be such a comparative framework. One does not need to know what a just South African society would look like in order to be able to say that racial discrimination is unjust and that a situation where people are not discriminated against on the basis of their skin colour is better, or more just, than one in which people are discriminated against. In a situation of racial discrimination, people are not able to do or be what they might have reason to value, such as being treated with respect, studying at good universities or exercising a certain profession. A transformed situation in which people can enjoy these valuable capabilities is better and therefore more just because it provides more opportunities for people to do or be what they have reason to value or, in Nussbaum's interpretation, because it provides more opportunities for people to enjoy central human capabilities.

In sum, the normative language of the capability approach offers a framework to judge a situation, and that judgement leads to a certain type of action to transform that situation. As discussed in Chapter 2, the type of information one uses for judging situations matters for social action. Whether one judges how well India is doing as a country from the perspective of income or capabilities, such as, the ability for children to be well nourished, this will lead to different types of policies. While the capability approach orients action in a certain direction, it is not prescriptive about what types of actions are best. There are many ways to reduce the same injustice, and this will be context-dependent. How does one reduce child malnutrition in India? There are hundreds of ways to do so, including providing a midday meal at schools, improving the education of mothers, creating employment opportunities and controlling food prices. The capability approach leaves it up to social actors in their given context to frame the most appropriate actions to provide opportunities for people to live well. It may be that in one context, the best way for people to have the opportunity for meaningful employment is by creating cooperative enterprises with workers owning the capital and all having a say in the management of the company. In other contexts, this action may not be suitable and it may be that shareholder behaviour regulation may be the most appropriate action to secure opportunities for dignified employment.

Within a capability view of justice, there are no set principles which guarantee that a society will be just. It is up to social actors themselves, in their specific context, to discuss through public reasoning processes what constitutes an injustice – in other words, to identify which valuable capabilities people are deprived of – and to discuss the most appropriate actions to remedy the injustice they face. What are the capabilities that people living along the Changuinola River in Panama have reason to value? What actions can they take so that they have opportunities to enjoy these valuable capabilities? The answer to these questions, a capability view of justice argues, lies in the nature and quality of public reasoning processes, what it includes or excludes as its object, who it includes or excludes as its subject and how it is conducted. As an open-ended normative language, the capability approach can, and often has to, incorporate vocabularies from other theories, such as theories on deliberative democracy with their account of the conditions under which the public reasoning process is fair or just,[2] or critical theories of justice with their multidimensional account of justice in terms of recognition, distribution and representation.[3]

Justice and public reasoning

In many ways, the capability language retains the 'general Rawlsian position that the interpretation of justice is linked with public reasoning' (Sen 2006: 215), but shifts the focus from procedural principles to comparative assessment and ranking of states of affairs, which provide the benchmark with which to assess the quality of public reasoning. *The Idea of Justice* is replete with references about the importance of reasoning for overcoming unjust situations. To cite one of many such references, which tellingly underlines one crucial aspect of Sen's understanding of public reasoning, namely the ability to listen to divergent points of views and see the world from someone else's perspective: 'When we try to determine how justice can be advanced, there is a basic need for public reasoning, involving arguments coming from different quarters and divergent perspectives' (Sen 2009: 392).

Of course, disagreement permeates public reasoning processes, and people do not readily engage with other people's perspectives and try to see the world from their point of view. The suffragettes had to encounter a lot of what Sen calls 'unreason' from men, who had their own 'reasons' to keep women outside the economic, social and political sphere. All men were not disposed to enter the perspectives of women's lives and seek to understand their arguments from their viewpoints.

The reality of clashing reasons does not, however, rule out the possibility of people changing their views on the basis of accepting others' reasons. This can be because the reasons for holding certain views are often based on prejudices that do not withstand critical scrutiny. Nonetheless, persistent reasoning, Sen argues, can overcome 'unreason', as he writes:

> The pervasiveness of unreason presents good grounds for scepticism about the practical effectiveness of reasoned discussion of confused social subjects. . . . This particular scepticism of the reach of reasoning does not yield any ground for not using reason to the extent one can, in pursuing the idea of justice. . . . Unreason is mostly not the practice of doing without reasoning altogether, but of relying on a very primitive and very defective reasoning. There is hope in this since bad reasoning can be confronted by better reasoning.
>
> *(Sen 2009: xvii–xviii)*

In his recent book with Jean Drèze on India, Sen continues to underline that listening to everyone's point of view, from their perspective, is a critical component of the exercise of public reasoning. They discuss especially the role of the media in enabling everyone's view to be heard and in enabling people to understand the lives and problems of others. Drèze and Sen (2013: 266) illustrate the poor contribution of the Indian media to public reasoning with the fact that rural issues, which affect the majority of Indians, only get an average of 2 per cent of coverage in the main media. There is a lot of coverage about fashion, gastronomy, cricket and space missions but very little, if any, about the spread of malnutrition (India has the largest mal-nourished population in the world) and the lack of basic sanitation infra-structure (half of the Indian population does not have access to a toilet).

This, they argue, is a 'failure of public reasoning' (Drèze and Sen 2013: 269). Bringing the voices of those who do not have the opportunity to be well-nourished or to defecate privately into the public arena and getting them heard by those who are well nourished and enjoy all the mod cons of modern life, would be a first step towards making India a more just society.

A similar argument can be made in the Panama case of the hydroelectric dam described in Chapter 1. The dispossession of Naso land and the injustice they suffered – injustice being defined as the denial of opportunities they have to live the kind of life they have reason to value – reflects a failure of public reasoning. The perspective of the people who lived on the land on which the dam was built has not been taken into account. The views of the Naso people have not been featured in the decision to create a market institution for people in Northern countries to offset their carbon emissions by paying for renewable energy projects in the Southern hemisphere (the Clean Development Mechanism), nor have their views been heard by the Panamanian government. The view that the government listened to was the minority view, which agreed with its decision. Other perspectives on the desirability of building a dam were sidelined, either by exclusion from the decision-making process – consultations were set at such places and with such notice that few Naso could participate – or by intimidation – the police shooting on people demonstrating against the dam.

From a capability view of justice, a successful reasoning process would be one which led to actions such that all the subjects involved, the Naso people, the other citizens of Panama and people in Northern countries, would have had opportunities to do or be what they have reason to value in their contexts. Obviously, there may be a clashing of reasons. The inhabitants of Panama City may have reason to value conducting activities requiring more electricity; the Naso people may have reason to value living off their land; and Northern people may have reason to value an energy-intensive lifestyle and offset their carbon emissions elsewhere. Nonetheless, the argument goes, a common agreement can be found on how best to distribute resources and use the land. This may include revising the reasons for which one valued certain doings and beings, such as living a lifestyle with high carbon footprints, after confronting one's reasons with other people's reasons to live a sustainable lifestyle; or revising the reasons for which one opposed the dam project after being confronted with the government's and company's reasons for the dam and the benefits it would bring.

Power, domination and intimidation do, of course, permeate the public reasoning process, as Drèze and Sen have widely illustrated in the case of India and the immense power that the most privileged have to shape what is discussed in the media and what gets priority in policy. That the Indian government spent more than 1.5 per cent of its GDP on subsidizing fertilizers in 2008–9, and the same amount on providing health care, is a gross manifestation of the power that agro-businesses yield in policymaking over those of the hundreds of millions of Indians who are malnourished and the thousands who die each month of easily preventable diseases (Drèze and Sen 2013: 83). Similarly in Panama, the power of corporations in shifting policy priorities, and indeed influencing what people have reason to value, is also at play.[4] The Colombian company building the dam reports that it employs 366 people from the Naso indigenous peoples and that it has signed an agreement to spend US$2.3 million in social projects with the Naso community.[5] This undoubtedly changes the dynamics of the reasoning process and the kinds of lives they have reason to value.

Within a capability view of justice, as Sen presents it, seeking to make unjust situations less unjust does not require complete agreement on how to transform the reality and on the reasons for doing so. As he writes, 'Judgements about justice have to take on board the task of accommodating different kinds of reasons and evaluative concerns' (Sen 2009: 395). People may give different reasons for removing gender discrimination in the workplace, whether on the ground of greater productivity or human rights and non-discrimination. People may give different reasons for tackling climate change, whether on the ground of cost effectiveness – not investing in clean technology now will result in greater economic losses in the future as the Stern Report on the Economics of Climate Change highlighted – or on the ground of protecting nature in its own right. For Sen, it does not matter that we have different reasons for doing certain actions, as long as we can agree on what action to take, this is sufficient to start reducing injustice. Even if there are fundamental disagreements about how to tackle climate change, there is partial agreement about the ranking that a world with less carbon emissions is better than the current one, and this is sufficient to galvanize action to make the situation better or more just. As Sen (2009: 394) puts it, 'If the importance of public reasoning has been one of the major concerns of this book, so has been the need to accept the plurality of reasons that may be sensibly accommodated in an exercise of evaluation'.

In many cases, Sen argues, it is sufficient to stop at a partial ranking without having to look for complete agreement over all rankings. Thus reasoned partial agreement that one state of affairs is more just than another is all that is needed to start making the world less unjust. We do not need to agree about how to rank wind turbines, hydroelectric power, solar panels or nuclear energy as the most environmentally friendly way of generating energy in order to start taking concrete steps to reduce carbon emissions.

We can at least agree that adopting recycling policies or subsidies for house insulation is a step in the right direction.

Within a capability view of justice, it is up to public reasoning processes within each context to determine not only what constitutes valuable beings and doings but also what constitutes appropriate institutional arrangements to ensure that people have opportunities to do or be what they have reason to value. So, as to the question whether the Clean Development Mechanism is a just institutional arrangement, a capability view of justice would say that the answer is context-dependent and depends on whether it allows all of the subjects affected by it to be or do what they have reason to value. For the Naso people of Panama, this arrangement is clearly unjust as it has led to the loss of their autonomy over their territory. For the Panama government, it is just because it gives them the necessary economic resources to produce renewable energy. One can already see here that, in order to illuminate concrete social realities and offer insights for remedying injustice, a capability view of justice would need to be interpreted in a certain way and not be left to reasoning processes alone, essential as they are, to solve conflicting views.

A normative language to transform situations

Like its account of wellbeing, a capability-based view of justice is open to interpretation. Sen framed his account of justice with a specific audience in mind, the academic audience who uses Rawls's theory of justice as a reference point for conceptualizing social justice. But when the keywords of the language are spoken in different contexts, they acquire a different set of meanings and applications.

A partial theory of justice

Martha Nussbaum was the first capability theorist to depart from Sen's original account. As discussed in the previous chapter, whereas Sen situated the evaluation space of wellbeing in the capabilities people have reason to value and left to public debate the task of specifying valuable capabilities, Nussbaum argued that, because public reasoning processes were not immune from power abuse and therefore people may come to value capabilities which may be harmful to them, one had to specify which capabilities were valuable. She went beyond Sen's comparative account of justice by linking her list of central human capabilities to constitutionally guaranteed fundamental entitlements, and by holding governments responsible for securing central human capabilities (Nussbaum 2003, 2007).

Her interpretation of a capability view of justice, what she calls the 'capabilities approach', is more prescriptive than Sen's, for it gives citizens some framework to hold their governments responsible and accountable for what they should do: to protect a set of fundamental individual entitlements.[6] However, there is a large scope for both Nussbaum's and Sen's interpretations to converge. Considering the case of bodily integrity, Nussbaum's account holds it a valuable capability irrespective of whether public reasoning processes hold it valuable, for they may be dominated by patriarchal norms, which may make women not value such capability. Sen's account will not take an explicit position on whether bodily integrity is a valuable capability until its 'valuableness' is underpinned by public debate and reasoning, such as when the population of India became outraged at the rape and murder of a student on a Delhi bus in December 2012 and put bodily integrity high on the policy agenda.[7]

While Nussbaum adds to Sen's capability view of justice a stronger prescriptive role for governments, her interpretation remains similar to Sen's in its endorsement of ethical individualism. Each person has to be seen as an end in him- or herself. Structures such as the caste system and patriarchy, and groups such as religious and self-help groups are important in determining capability outcomes, but as far as justice is concerned, what matters is not what a structure or group is doing but how *each* individual is doing and the impact of these structures and groups on the lives of each individual. However, Drèze and Sen's latest book on India departs from this position by providing a vivid description of the 'grip of inequality' on Indian society (Drèze and Sen 2013: 213), whether at gender, caste or class level, even acknowledging that these entrenched structures of inequality severely mould the public reasoning process, which in turn reinforces the persistence of these inequalities.[8] From Drèze and Sen's work on India, one can notice that a slightly different interpretation of a capability view of justice unfolds from the one contained in Sen's *Idea of Justice* and in Nussbaum's writings. Through the analysis of some concrete actions for removing injustice, that is, removing obstacles which prevent people from enjoying the sets of beings and doings that they have reason to value, the remainder of this chapter outlines this interpretation of a capability view of justice.

Let us first consider the case of actions oriented at reducing child malnutrition in India. A capability view of justice demands, first, an evaluation of states of affairs in the capability space and makes the judgement that a situation where more people are adequately nourished is more just. It then demands inclusive reasoning processes in which all parties are heard in order to reach a collective decision about what should be done to enable more people to enjoy these basic capabilities. Drèze and Sen (2002: 336–40) discuss one specific obstacle which prevents children from being well nourished: the government support of a minimum price for food producers, which has led to massive grain stocks being left to rot, as the government had to buy surplus food to maintain prices. This situation of rotting food and high levels of child malnutrition is unjust, as it is clear that a programme of food distribution from these government-maintained stocks would provide more opportunities for children to be well nourished.

Drèze and Sen diagnose the cause of this unjust situation in the power imbalance between large-scale and subsistence farmers. The former are well organized politically and have their interest represented in the democratic sphere. The remedy for such injustice, they argue, is better public reasoning, in the sense of a democratic process where all voices are equally heard. Drèze and Sen (2011, 2013) highlight another instance of the capability for children to be well nourished being threatened by a failure of the democratic process: members of the Indian Parliament received letters from the Biscuit Manufacturers' Association praising the benefits of manufactured food and urging them to replace the school meal programme, up to this point cooked by local people using local food, with their products. This corporate influence on the political process was eventually exposed in the media thanks to the Right to Information Act.[9]

Diagnosing unjust structures

When comparing Sen's *Idea of Justice* and his collaborative works with Jean Drèze on the political economy of India, one notices some major differences. In the latter work, there is a strong connection between failure of individuals to enjoy the most fundamental things of life and the democratic malfunctioning of the Indian state. Thus, individual capability outcomes and quality of democratic structure, especially the power relations between different groups and the grip of inequality, are important pieces of information to evaluate states of affairs. There is also the critical role of political organization. In the former work, however, Sen is reluctant for 'group capabilities', such as the opportunities subsistence farmers and landless labourers have to make their concerns heard as a group and not as individuals, to become part of a discourse on justice. As noted in the previous chapter, he argued that it was sufficient to 'value a person's ability to take part in the life of a society' (Sen 2009: 246). But in the case of the inability of a large number of Indians to enjoy basic capabilities such as being adequately nourished, it is not the individual daily labourer's ability to participate in democratic politics which will make a difference to his life but the ability of daily labourers to participate in political decisions as a group or political organization. As Drèze and Sen conclude their analysis of India and its contradictions, to remedy injustice, they say, is 'partly a matter of political organization' but 'there is also the important role for a clear-headed understanding of the extensive reach and peculiar nature of deprivation and inequality in India' (Drèze and Sen 2013: 287). And such 'clear-headed understanding' involves a structural analysis, for the nature of capability deprivation lies in a failure of economic, social and political structures. One can indeed not give an account of the extent of capability deprivation in India without giving an account of how these structures function, as Drèze and Sen (2013) have forcefully demonstrated.

A capability view of justice needs therefore to take into account the wider economic, political and social structures in which individuals and groups operate. The political philosopher Hannah Arendt identified three kinds of structures which are essential for human life to develop (Arendt 1958): those belonging to the cultural sphere which enable humans to adopt a language and set of behavioural norms and practices to communicate with others; those belonging to the economic sphere which enable human needs to be met, through production, distribution and consumption; and those belonging to the political sphere which enable humans to act and shape their destiny through their own free action. Each of these structures are the product of interpersonal relations but have also acquired an existence on their own, which is not easily amenable to change. They do indeed exercise a 'grip' on society, as Drèze and Sen (2013) characterized the influence of gender, caste and class inequality on Indian society.

There is currently a global economic structure, which is premised on minimizing production costs and maximizing profits. It is supported by economic actors who act according to these premises. Yet, it is very difficult for economic actors to engage in economic exchange on the basis of other premises such as paying wages above what other companies pay in the sector and selling products for the sake of maintaining the business and guaranteeing employment instead of maximizing profits. Similarly for political structures, they do acquire an existence beyond the reach of any individual. Nazism was the product of interpersonal relations. It is the German people who brought Hitler to power, yet, once national-socialism was in place, it became very difficult to engage with the German political structures outside the framework of national-socialism. The disconnection between structures and individual actions and reasoning can be such that an individual person may no longer realize that his or her actions are bad. He or she may even be led to act in a way which he or she profoundly disapproves of but has no agency to act in other way, or at the immense cost of his or her life (Deneulin et al. 2006).

The reality of structural injustice does not, however, detract from individual responsibility. It is individual human beings who internalize the unjust structure, reproduce it by their actions or stay silent. Let us take the example of the economic structure surrounding the fishing industry in Mar del Plata in Argentina.[10] In the 1970s, the government gave incentives for large-scale fishing companies to operate by lifting its ban on large trawlers. Fishermen who so far had been fishing in family enterprises internalized the values of the economic structure that the more fish they caught the better, even if it was far beyond meeting their family economic needs (responsibility by internalization). By internalizing these values, they contributed to building an economic structure in which it became impossible for sustainable family fishing to cover a family's needs, for they could not compete with the bigger businesses. Even those who did not agree with the values of large-scale industrial fishing had to comply with it in order to survive economically (responsibility by reproduction). But opting out of the structure and finding another source of employment outside the fishing sector is also contributing to reinforcing the structure of unsustainable fishing (responsibility by omission).

This interpretation of a capability view of justice includes, on the one hand, an account of valuable capabilities in order to diagnose that valuable capability is missing and, on the other, an account of the quality of the structures which underpin human life and the extent to which they allow people to live well on a shared planet. An unjust situation is not merely about individuals being unable to enjoy some valuable sets of beings and doings. It is also, and most fundamentally, about economic, political and socio-cultural structures being corrupted and deviated from their purpose: structuring life in common so that each, and all, may live well together on a shared planet. The question of just institutions or just structures is therefore not redundant, as Sen had once claimed in his *Idea of Justice*. Judging whether structures or institutions are just or good, that is, whether they provide the conditions for a good life in common, is central to the idea of justice. This was actually Nussbaum's earlier interpretation of a capability view of justice, to which the next section turns.

Reasoning and the common good

When Nussbaum first started to work on her interpretation of a capability view of justice in the late 1980s, she placed her capabilities approach within the Aristotelian ethical and political tradition. Her central human capabilities were seen as constituents of a human life that all humans share as being worthwhile. Human life has a *telos* or a goal: performing well or functioning

well in the various experiences of our humanity (hunger, emotions, affiliation, reasoning, play, bodily health, sexuality and others). People are free
to choose how to function well in each of these experiences, and they need
structuring material and social conditions to do so (Nussbaum 1988, 1990,
1992, 1993). Taking the case of the experience of hunger, people are free
to decide what 'being adequately nourished' consists of, and they need
a natural environment to grow food and an economic environment to
guarantee sustainable farming. The government has special responsibility to
create the structuring conditions for people to live good human lives.[11]

Nussbaum singles out two central human capabilities, affiliation and
practical reasoning, which infuse all others, for better or for worse. Children
need relationships for their physical and emotional development. These
relationships can be based on mutual love and self-giving or based on
contempt and self-interest. The type of relationships in which children grow
will significantly affect their cognitive and emotional abilities. Taking
affiliation beyond the family level, the type of government and political
structure in which children grow also structures, for better or worse, the
capabilities people have to live well. If a child grows in a democratic country
with a welfare state or a dictatorship without access to basic social services,
this will strongly affect the opportunities the child has to be or do certain
valuable things, such as playing with his or her friends or going to school.

On this Aristotelian interpretation of a capability view of justice,
affiliation is not a mere 'capability', something one needs to be given the
opportunity for but can choose not to make use of. It is a constitutive part
of what human life is, beyond choice.[12] There is no choice about the very
fact of being in relation with other people. Even if one chooses to live a life
of seclusion on a remote island, one is still related to the natural environment
and therefore to people elsewhere and what they choose to do in their
relations to nature. Affiliation is constitutive of human living, but the way
one affiliates is subject to a lesser or greater extent to choice. This recognition of the architectonic role of affiliation within the language of the
capability approach leads to an important difference of interpretation with
Sen's.

The fundamental anthropological reality of affiliation means that one's
own good is never pursued alone. It is co-dependent on a common good,
a good constituted by the relationships one engages with. Within this
relational anthropological vision of human life, the good of the community
formed by human relationships and the good of each individual in these
relationships are mutually implicating (Deneulin and Townsend 2007,
Hollenbach 2002). Let us consider the example of freedom of speech. On
the one hand, it is only individuals who speak. But yet, freedom of speech

is not an individual property; it is a good owned by a society as a whole and not by any individual. The individual freedom of speech is a truly common good because it rests on:[13] (1) people viewing each other in a way which recognizes that it is good for each person to speak his or her own mind; (2) people acting towards each other with certain attitudes (respect for diverging opinions) because they view each other in a way which recognizes freedom of opinion and speech as good; and (3) on people coming together in public dialogue to give concrete definitions of what a free society consists of. That Germany has different freedom of speech laws regarding the Holocaust from the United States is an expression that freedom of speech is a good which can be enjoyed by individuals because it is first a common good, a good truly held in common and by no individual in particular.

An objection to this interpretation of a capability-based account of justice is that, considering human lives and communities as teleologically structured (Blackledge and Knight 2011), that is, judging human actions according to their contribution to an end, whether they provide the structuring conditions for each person to live well on a shared planet, raises concerns about authoritarianism. Who is to define what living well is and what a good life in common is? This objection can, however, be refuted if one holds a vision of the common good as something essentially contested (Keys 2006, Tyler 2006). That the human good, and its structuring conditions, is not fixed and set once and for all, does not rule out the possibility for the human good to be the ethical horizon of public reasoning processes and decisions.

Within this interpretation of a capability view of justice, one's agency, one's ability to act and make decisions, has a *telos*, the human good and the structuring material and social conditions of that good. Freedom and responsibility towards each other and the environment become synonymous.[14] Public reasoning becomes a matter of discussing the nature of what a good human life consists of and what kinds of social and material conditions are needed for humans to live well with each other on a shared planet.

Sen's capability-based account of justice stops short of situating reasoning processes explicitly within a teleological horizon. In *The Idea of Justice*, the activity of reasoning does not have the explicit end of the provision of the conditions in which every person can live a good life in common. Notwithstanding, one could say that the examples Sen gave about reasoning processes overcoming injustice, women's struggles against patriarchy or abolition of slavery, were based on a teleological view of the reasoning process. It was a vision of human dignity, equality of all human beings irrespective of sex or colour of skin, which guided the reasoning processes and served as a benchmark for overcoming 'unreason'. When the suffragettes confronted the 'bad' reasoning of men and argued that women had equal political and civil rights, their reasoning bore upon the question of whether a society's cultural, economic and political structures were enabling each human being, including women, to live well, or whether they were perverted from that aim. When Martin Luther King confronted the reasoning of the American society at the time, that black people were different from white and therefore should not have the same political and economic opportunities, he did so on the grounds of the *telos* of the human good, a vision of human dignity in which all are equal, whether black or white, man or woman. The material and social conditions in the United States did not support that aim. A reordering of the social, political and economic structures was required so that all may live well as human beings, irrespective of the colour of their skin. The ability of black people to enjoy valuable sets of beings and doings, such as being university educated and marrying a person of their choice could not be enjoyed by each individual American person unless it rested on how American people related to each other and how this was expressed through the economic, social and political structures. Ultimately, the ability of each human being to live well rests upon the extent to which other people engage in practical reasoning and exercise their agency in a responsible way in view of the good of others, and the environment, on which their own good depends, but it is a good which is endlessly redefined.[15]

The resistance movements of indigenous people to protect their land from destruction caused by the exploitation of natural resources illustrate this link between justice and deliberation about the good life in common. Their struggles for justice are, foremost, struggles to redefine the vision of the common good held by the society at large and the structuring conditions which guarantee it. The next section discusses the struggles of indigenous peoples in Ecuador to illustrate the argument that opportunities people have to be or do what they have reason to value and just structures are intimately linked, and to ground an interpretation of a capability view of justice which considers living well and acting justly as two sides of the same coin.

Acting justly and living well

The environmental degradation caused by the extractive industry has been a concern in the public arena in Ecuador ever since oil extraction started in the 1960s. It is in the 1990s, however, that the issue became a central public concern with the increase in extractive activities,[16] and the consequent increase in social and political mobilizations against the dispossession of land and environmental damage which mining concessions involved. In the case of Ecuador, these mobilizations gathered around the idea of *sumak kwasay*, which broadly translates from Kichwa as a 'system of knowledge and living based on the communion of humans and nature and on the spatial-temporal-harmonious totality of existence' (Walsh 2010: 18). Similar mobilizations took place in neighbouring Bolivia around the idea of *suma quamaña*, Aymara for 'living in harmony with the whole of social relations [including the environment] with an attitude of thanksgiving' (Albó 2008). These ideas have been brought together under the Spanish term *buen vivir*, which, more than 'living well', means living in harmony with each other and the natural environment (Gudynas 2011a, b).

There are complex reasons as to why these ideas have taken political prominence. Among them is the specific political context of Ecuador, which, with Bolivia, has offered a nurturing ground for indigenous peoples to mobilize politically and acquire political power. Yashar (2005) highlights in particular the formation of peasant organizations in the 1950s and 1960s under a socialist state which allowed groups to organize along corporatist interests, and the freedom of speech and expression granted in the 1990s under a liberal state which allowed peasants to redefine themselves as indigenous and to demand the states recognize them as such. Another reason is the specific experience of indigenous peoples of dispossession of land and environmental degradation caused by economic policies which exploit nature as a way of generating economic resources. It is precisely this vision of the 'good life in common', which sees the 'good life' as one in which people seek material pursuits in a relation of domination with the environment, that these mobilizations seek to replace by bringing the idea of *buen vivir* to the core of political debates and public policy.

This redefinition of the 'good life in common' through the idea of *buen vivir* is not confined to the boundaries of the struggles of indigenous peoples in the Andes. Because it is based on the premise that to live well is to live in harmony with each other and the environment, the political project of indigenous communities in the Andes is linked at the international level to other social movements which share a similar relational anthropology. Among these are most notably religious traditions but also the movement towards de-growth and voluntary simplicity (Martínez-Alier *et al.* 2010, Thomson 2011, van Dijk 2012), although these have not yet engaged with economic and political structures on the scale that indigenous movements in the Andes have.

The idea of *buen vivir* filtrated into political discourses in Ecuador when the confederation of indigenous organizations, Confederación de Nacionalidades Indígenas de Ecuador (CONAIE) formed the political party Pachacutik and ran for elections in 1996. Subsequently, President Correa and his party Allianza País took over the indigenous demands for a plurinational state and recognition for autonomy over their territory (Jameson 2011).[17] *Buen vivir* progressively penetrated the political structure and has become the rallying mantra of the Ecuadorian government since Correa's elections in 2007, at least in its discourses and external relations.

The translation of this vision of harmonious relationships between people and their environment into reality is, however, fraught with conflicts, disagreements and contradictions. In 2008, Ecuador adopted a constitution oriented towards *buen vivir*, which includes the right of Nature. In 2009, it drafted a national plan for *buen vivir*, which includes a wide range of objectives such as increasing access to education at all levels, reducing foreign participation in domestic consumption, reducing malnutrition, making the tax structure more distributive, reducing land concentration, reducing ecological footprints and increasing the role of small and medium-size companies in the economy. But behind the policy discourses and intentions, the reality proves to be rather different.

In contrast to what is stated in the *buen vivir* National Plan, the role of the extractive industry in the economy has not decreased and more mining concessions on indigenous land have been granted, with reports of the government dividing people to win support for its mining activities.[18] The pioneering Fund to compensate for not exploiting the Yasuní National Park was abandoned in August 2013 and the exploitation of the Amazon region is deepening.[19] There may be the argument that the oil is bringing more government revenues to invest in health, but the Ecuadorian Medical Association has expressed concerns that the substantial increase in investment in health during Correa's government, from US$371 million in 2004 to US$1.6 billion in 2012, has been wasteful and is not addressing the social causes of ill health, and that the greater labour flexibility, privatization and outsourcing of services introduced in the health sector, is going against the nation's health.[20] The scope for free public reasoning is being tightened by the blurring of the executive, legislative and judicial powers.[21] *Buen vivir* is increasingly becoming a foreign policy propaganda which does not match the reality of national policy, a far cry from the original demands of indigenous peoples to live following their specific vision of human relations, economic exchange and relation to land – as a consequence of this, indigenous organizations have cut their link with the government. But despite these setbacks, the political and social mobilization around *buen vivir* offers some important insights as to why a capability-based view of justice can be used to analyse and help transform unjust social realities, and why questions of justice are closely connected to questions of wellbeing, and vice-versa.

First, the capability language gives tools to judge whether a situation is just or unjust by offering a comparative framework. Do economic policies which give incentives to the extractive industry provide more opportunities for people to do or be what they have reason to value? Do Ecuadorians have more opportunities to be healthy, to be educated, to engage in political participation without fear of intimidation, to have freedom of speech, to live in a non-polluted environment and to live in relation to animals and the world of nature (to take a few of Nussbaum's central capabilities)? Do ecosystems have the opportunity to reproduce themselves, as Ecuadorians have come to value through processes of public reasoning the 'right of nature' and rights of ecosystems to be protected?

In addition to an evaluation of outcomes, a capability-based view of justice also includes in its assessment the nature of public reasoning and its quality, whether it is oriented towards providing the conditions for people to do or be what they have reason to value. In the case of Ecuador, this would entail doing a careful analysis of the public reasoning process and configuration of power between different social and political actors, and how this public reasoning process, within or outside state structures, through dialogue or confrontation, leads to the transformation of existing social, economic and political structures or the creation of new ones. What power do indigenous organizations such as CONAIE and ECUARANI have, compared to Chinese mining companies in influencing mining and energy policy? What is the influence of the Ecuadorian public debt on government policy decisions? How is the constitutional right of the right of Nature implemented? These are some of the questions that an analysis of the Ecuadorian situation would ask when judged through the prism of the normative language of the capability approach. Using the language also highlights that the building of a more just society and establishing the conditions which enable each person to live well is a never achieved process. It is always in the making, and unmaking.

In the interpretation of a capability view of justice presented here, using the language will also involve making an assessment of social, economic and political arrangements, and how the Ecuadorian society is structured towards enabling people to live well. Just actions, or actions aimed at transforming existing institutional arrangements to improve people's lives, such as reducing the role of the extractive industry in the economy and extending health coverage or opening access to higher education to groups hitherto excluded, are intrinsically connected to how living well is understood. Within a capability view of justice, just actions are the ones which transform the social, economic and political reality such that people are able to function well as human beings on a shared planet. However, just actions are not imposed, it is social actors themselves who endlessly redefine what it means to live well on a shared planet, and how to create the necessary conditions for this vision to become reality in their own specific contexts. The indigenous social movements in Ecuador have chosen to do so under the banner of *buen vivir* and to change social, economic and political structures towards greater harmonious relations between people and the natural environment.

This chapter has argued that there are structuring conditions for living well and that these lie in the quality of relations between individuals, whether at the economic, social and political level, and between individuals and nature. When indigenous people suffer ill health caused by extractive activities, actions to remedy that injustice (seen as lacking opportunity to be healthy) require a transformation of the economic and political relationships behind health outcomes (Valencia 2012b). This includes a transformation of the set of economic relations, from exploiting humans and nature for the sake of profits to putting profits at the service of human life and nature, and a transformation of the way humans relate to nature, from exploitation and domination to stewardship.

Amartya Sen presented a new moral approach in the social sciences to analyse the social reality from the perspective of freedom, in its dual aspects of wellbeing and agency. The central question to ask, Sen (1985: 195) argued, was: 'What kind of a life is she [a person] leading? What does she succeed in doing and in being?'. This book has gone one step further and argued that the answer to that question is closely connected to the answer to another question: how do people relate to each other in their economic, social and political relations? Are they acting in a way which enables their fellow human beings to live well or 'be or do what they have reason to value'? What kinds of actions do social, political and economic structures facilitate? Do they facilitate just actions? This is what the next chapter will examine in the light of two case studies from Latin America.

Notes

1 See Brighouse and Robeyns (2010) for a discussion on primary goods and capabilities as the informational basis of justice.
2 See Crocker (2006, 2008) for an integration of theories of deliberative democracy with the capability approach.
3 Fraser (2008) argues that representation constitutes the most fundamental dimension of justice and that overcoming injustice requires removing the obstacles, whether economic, social or political, which prevent people from participating as peers in social life. See Robeyns (2003) and Pereira (2013) for an integration of critical theory with the capability approach.
4 This point about the power of multinational corporations and the advertising industry in shaping what 'people have reason to value', was first made by Evans (2002).
5 Information taken from a promotional video made by the company EPM entitled 'Bonyic, empleo para el pueblo indígena Naso en Panamá', available in Spanish only, on YouTube.

6 See the book symposium on Nussbaum's book *Creating Capabilities* (2011), edited by Clark (2013).

7 Drèze and Sen (2013) highlight that, despite the rape of women – especially of scheduled caste by the high caste – being widespread in India, the event suddenly made bodily integrity and violence against women a high policy priority because the victim was from the middle classes.

8 They consider particularly the case of the media and how, by its dominance of the high caste and upper middle classes, it continues to reproduce the grip of inequality. As they put it: 'The media is not only moulded by the unequal society, its potentially corrective role in Indian social and political thinking is made more difficult by the society that has moulded it' (Drèze and Sen 2013: 266).

9 The Act was passed in 2005 and anyone can apply to demand access to government documents and information. The government is legally obliged to give them within 30 days (Drèze and Sen 2013: 100).

10 I am grateful to Juan Martín Molinari for this argument and example.

11 Nussbaum has now departed from grounding her account of justice on a comprehensive conception of the good. See Nussbaum (2013) for her critique of such interpretation of a capability-based view of justice.

12 See also Wolff and De-Shalit (2013) who argue that 'affiliation' is best understood as a functioning and not capability. They interpret capability as freedom to achieve a functioning in one's own way and not as freedom to achieve a functioning or not, which seems to be the interpretation favoured by Sen and Nussbaum.

13 I am indebted to Colin Tyler for this example and argument.

14 See Ballet *et al.* (2007) and Pelenc *et al.* (2013) for a discussion on freedom and responsibility within the capability approach.

15 See Sandel (2009) for an account of justice based on the common good and the argument that questions about justice cannot be separated from questions about the good life and the good society. Chapter 5 further discusses this teleological interpretation of agency in relation to Sen's recent account of 'enlightened agency'.

16 The share of the extractive industry in Ecuador's GDP rose from an average of 13.3 per cent between 1990 and 2007 to 23 per cent in 2007 (Bebbington and Bebbington-Humphreys 2011: 143).

17 For a detailed analysis of the transformation of indigenous social movements in political parties in Ecuador, and Latin America, see Lee Van Cott (2005).

18 See the *Guardian* article on 4 March 2013 entitled 'Ecuador: Amazon families split over lure of oil money' at http://www.guardian.co.uk/world/2013/mar/05/ecuador-amazon-split-oil-money.

19 See the article by Amazon Watch of March 2013 entitled 'Ecuador's Amazon for sale in Beijing' at http://amazonwatch.org/news/2013/0325-ecuadors-amazon-for-sale-in-beijing.

20 Data taken from a commentary by Maurico Torres-Tovar and Pol De Vos published in March 2013 entitled 'The Correa Phenomenon: Between buen vivir and neo-developmentalism' at http://e.itg.be/ihp/archives/correa-phenomenon-ecuador-buen-vivir-neo-developmentalism. The letter of discontent of the Ecuadorian Medical Federation, which was once public, is now no longer available in the public domain.

21 See the article by the American Society (October 2012) entitled 'Concerns arise over new constitutional court judges in Ecuador' at http://www.as-coa.org/articles/concerns-arise-over-new-constitutional-court-judges-ecuador. From personal interviews conducted in June 2012 in Ecuador, there are concerns that the government is increasing its grip on the media and reports of journalists being sacked when criticizing its policies.

4

ASSESSING AND TRANSFORMING SOCIAL REALITIES

Using the language

The book has so far described the capability approach as an open-ended normative language with which to assess situations from the perspective of human freedom, in its dual dimensions of wellbeing and agency. It has argued that, by doing so, it provides some frame for social and political action. The book has also emphasized that the language is not fixed and has a rather limited vocabulary. It contains a few keywords which actors are free to combine, use and supplement the way they view the most appropriate for the context they seek to assess and transform. The language is dynamic in that the meaning of its keywords varies according to the reality in which it is spoken. Should freedom be about capability or functioning? Should valuable functionings be about a set of predetermined sets of beings and doings that are believed to be characteristic of a fulfilled human life, or should it be determined according to context?

The previous chapters have argued that the language has been deliberately left ambiguous and open to a variety of interpretations, but that this did not detract from it being powerfully useful when it comes to offering a different assessment of states of affairs, from income or resources to what people are able to be or do,[1] and to offering some outline of action for transforming that reality so that people can be or do what they have reason to value. This chapter illustrates how the language of the capability approach can be used in order to assess, and transform, two selected Latin American realities. The methodology adopted is moulded on the dual purpose of the language as interpreted earlier: to assess and transform states of affairs from the perspective of human freedom.

When it comes to assessing states of affairs and describing the reality that we see, there is obviously no view from nowhere. The same reality can be described in many different ways depending on where the person looking at the situation is coming from. For some, a demonstration against the granting of a concession for an open-pit mine can be seen as a disturbance of social order and an obstacle to progress, depriving the government of revenues needed for social services and public infrastructure. For others, the same demonstration can be seen as an expression of civil and political rights and a sign of progress, preserving the natural environment and human life for future generations.

The capability approach takes the normative standpoint that states of affairs are best assessed from the perspective of people's wellbeing and agency. What kind of lives are people able to live? Do they have opportunities to be or do what they have reason to value? In analysing some selected social realities, this chapter follows the practice of those working with the capability approach. Alkire (2008a) has argued that the choice of what information to include in the assessment of states of affairs and what counts as 'valuable' sets of being or doing depends on: data availability, assumptions about what is valuable (such as Nussbaum's list of central human capabilities), public consensus on what is valuable (such as the universal declaration on human rights) and ongoing deliberative participatory processes (what a group of people themselves decides to be valuable). Often, a combination of these will be used to select the relevant wellbeing dimensions and indicators.

But the reality is not assessed for the mere sake of assessment. It is assessed so that a judgement can be made about whether the reality can be less unjust. In that regard, the book has argued that assessing the quality of economic, social and political structures which underpin the extent to which people have opportunities to do or be what they have reason to value, was an integral component of the evaluation exercise. However, while the capability approach provides an evaluation framework to judge whether some situations are more just or unjust than others, it is not prescriptive about what kinds of actions would make them less unjust, and does not describe what just structures would look like. It maintains that a just society is an unattainable horizon. A state of affairs where each person is able to live well always escapes us. Nonetheless, that the reality of a fully just society is always beyond human reach, does not mean that reducing injustice is beyond reach. As Sen (2006) pointed out, one may never know what a 'just' American society will ever be but one knows that a public health-care system which does not exclude anyone on the ground of individual ability to pay will be more just, in the sense of enabling more people to live a long and healthy life, than current public health arrangements in the United States. That other injustices will always remain is not a reason for doing nothing about remedying a few of them. An American version of the British National Health Service may not remedy the injustice of racial discrimination and bring equal employment and educational opportunities for blacks and whites, but it will nonetheless make American society less unjust.

Within this background of offering a comparative framework for making societies less unjust while keeping the just society as an unattainable horizon, the language of the capability approach holds political processes of public reasoning as one of the central bones of its architecture. As Sen (2013b: 24) recently stated in the 2013 *Human Development Report*: 'Only the wearer may know where the shoe pinches, but pinch-avoiding arrangements cannot be effectively undertaken without giving voice to the people and giving them extensive opportunities for discussion'. Poor quality public reasoning processes, typically ones in which people are not able to express 'what ails their lives and what injustices they want to remove' (Sen 2013b: 24), often lie behind unjust situations and the lack of opportunities people have to be or do a set of valuable things. As Drèze and Sen (2013) discussed in the case of India, one of the major reasons behind the fact that hundreds of millions of Indians lack opportunities for basic human functionings, is the unequal structure of Indian society and their inability to make their voices heard in the political process. Therefore, when judging states of affairs, one has to pay special attention to the quality of the political structure and the power that some citizens, or some groups or organizations, command over others.

Two social realities have been selected to illustrate how the language of the capability approach can be used to assess and transform situations: the marginal urban areas of Buenos Aires in Argentina and the smelter town of La Oroya in Peru. The justification for their choice is threefold. First, each contains themes of relevance well beyond their context. The analysis of the slums of Buenos Aires has implications for other cities which have seen their slum areas grow in the last 20 years. The local Argentinian reality parallels the global trends of urbanization and rural migration.[2] The reality of the Peruvian smelter town highlights the tensions between employment opportunities and health in a context of resource extraction and environmental degradation. This local reality parallels the growth of extractive activities throughout the world and the apparent trade-offs between increasing demand for natural resources and environmental protection.[3] Second, both realities involve complex linkages between the local, national and global level. The 1990s economic liberalization decade at the global level[4] has deeply affected each of these local realities, as have also decisions taken by their national governments at some point in time. And third, both realities have been analysed by members of the academic community of the HDCA. As the argument of this book has matured through the many interactions over the years with other social scientists working with the capability approach as their analytical lens, building this chapter on existing empirical research is recognition of our academic interdependence. The analysis of the marginal urban areas of Buenos Aires builds upon research conducted by Eduardo Lépore, Silvia Lépore, Ann Mitchell, Jimena Macció and Emilse Rivero in Argentina, and the analysis of the smelter town of La Oroya builds upon the doctoral research of Areli Valencia in Peru.

The *villas* of Buenos Aires, Argentina

Villas miseria, or 'towns of misery', is the name given by Argentinians to the informal urban areas situated on vacant urban land occupied by migrant families. Their very naming is already a symptom of their reality of segregation from the rest of the city. They made their appearance in Buenos Aires in the 1930s when large-scale migration from rural to urban areas started. Their size increased with the import–substitution and industrialization policies pursued by the government in the 1960s and 1970s, which attracted more migrant workers from rural areas. The economic crisis of the 1980s, the 1990s economic liberalization policies which followed and the 2001 deep economic crisis which Argentina underwent, contributed to the continued growth of the *villas*. In 2010, nearly 6 per cent of the total population of the city of Buenos Aires were officially estimated to live in *villas*, a threefold increase from 1991.[5] What was once temporary occupation or settlement has become a permanent urban feature.

The kinds of lives people are living

The socio-demographic composition of the *villas* is a first signal of its segregation from the rest of the city. Their population is much younger than the rest of the city, is largely migrant and counts more children per family. According to 2010 national census data, the average age of the household head in the *villas* is 41, compared to 52 for the rest of the city; 64 per cent of the population are between 31 and 40 years old, compared to 34 per cent outside the *villas*. Nine out of ten household heads in the *villas* are not natives of Buenos Aires, and two out of three are from another Latin American country. Approximately 40 per cent of families in the *villas* have more than five members, compared to 8 per cent for the whole of city.

Women aged between 45 and 54 have on average 4.5 children, compared to 2.5 for women of the same age outside the *villas* (Macció and Lépore 2012: 59–60).

An assessment of how well people live in the *villas* compared to the rest of the city continues to mirror the reality of segregation. Following the practice of those using the capability approach for assessment, the next paragraphs combine information from available data, assumptions about what constitute valuable beings and doings, and what people in the *villas* themselves have reason to value being and doing. We start with data availability.

If one takes the 'capability to be adequately sheltered', Table 4.1 describes how the fact of living in a *villa* makes the enjoyment of this valuable capability much less likely. More than 17 per cent of houses in the *villas* do not have a toilet which connects to the public sewage network, compared to less than half a per cent for the city as a whole. Living in a *villa* makes one more than twice as likely to live in accommodation unsuitable for permanent living (such as living in a guesthouse, in a building not built for accommodation or in a shack). Nearly half of the people in the *villas* live in overcrowded conditions, defined as more than two people per room, a figure five times higher than for the rest of the city. Nearly 60 per cent of the inhabitants of the *villas* live in irregular housing tenancy (own the house but not land titles, occupy a building or live in work-related accommodation), compared to less than 10 per cent for those outside.

When one considers the 'capability to live long and healthy lives', Table 4.2 shows further that living in the *villas* means fewer opportunities to enjoy a valuable capability. The 2009 household survey for the city of Buenos Aires reports that nearly 80 per cent of those who live in the *villas* do not

TABLE 4.1 Indicators of the capability to be adequately sheltered in Buenos Aires

	Buenos Aires	Non-villas	Villas
Percentage of households without adequate sanitation	0.4	1.2	17.3
Percentage of households living in housing unsuitable for permanent living	4.6	4.3	10.6
Percentage of households with two people or more per room	8.2	6.2	49.7
Percentage of households in irregular housing tenancy	11.4	9.2	58.2

Source: Macció and Lépore (2012), on the basis of 2010 national census and 2009 household survey

TABLE 4.2 Indicators of the capability to live long and healthy lives in Buenos Aires

	Buenos Aires	Non-villas	Villas
Percentage of people without private medical insurance	27.0	21.0	78.0
Percentage of children without private medical insurance	18.0	15.0	77.0
Percentage of women (aged 14–49) declaring giving birth to stillborn child	2.6	–	8.4

Source: Macció and Lépore (2012), on the basis of 2010 national census and 2009 household survey

have private medical insurance and entirely rely on the public health service, compared to 21 per cent for those do not live in a *villa*. The difference is even more marked in the case of medical insurance coverage of children. Women in the *villas* are more than three times more likely to have a stillborn baby than women in Buenos Aires as a whole.

The pattern of segregation continues for the 'capability to be educated'. Table 4.3 shows that those who live in the *villas* are more than twice as likely to have an incomplete primary education. This difference is threefold when it comes to completing secondary education, although the gap diminishes for the overall adult population, suggesting that a large proportion of people may complete their secondary education after they are 25. The proportion of people with a tertiary degree is extremely small. Those in the *villas* almost entirely rely on public education, while less than half of the population outside the *villas* do so. A specific worry is the high percentage of young people, more than a quarter of the population aged between 18 and 24, who are neither working nor studying. This makes them particularly vulnerable to drug dealing and joining criminal gangs.

Table 4.4 continues the tale of segregation in relation to the capability to work. While youth employment is high throughout the city of Buenos Aires, it is higher in the *villas*. More than twice as many household heads in the *villas* are likely to be unemployed compared to the rest of the city. Female unemployment is also much higher in the *villas* than outside of them. Of those who are employed, a very large proportion of the people in the *villas*, nearly 80 per cent, are working in the informal sector. The employment they have is also more volatile and insecure. More than 20 per cent of those who have work are employed in the construction sector, a sector characteristically vulnerable to economic downturns and more health and safety insecure. The level of professional qualifications is also much lower

TABLE 4.3 Indicators of the capability to be educated in Buenos Aires

	Buenos Aires	Non-villas	Villas
Percentage of adolescents (aged 13–17) with incomplete primary education	14.0	13.0	26.0
Percentage of young people (aged 18–24) with incomplete secondary education	27.0	24.0	72.0
Average years of study of people aged 25 or over	12.5	–	8.0
Percentage of male adult population with incomplete secondary education	–	14.0	27.0
Percentage of female adult population with incomplete secondary education	–	17.0	29.0
Percentage of male adult population with tertiary degree	–	25.0	1.0
Percentage of female adult population with tertiary degree	–	22.0	1.0
Percentage of children (aged 6–12) who attend public education	53.4	49.2	92.6
Percentage of adolescents (aged 13–17) who attend public education	50.9	47.4	87.9
Percentage of young people (aged 18–24) who neither work nor study	9.0	8.0	28.0

Source: Macció and Lépore (2012), on the basis of 2010 national census and 2009 household survey

among the inhabitants of the *villas*. Nearly half of household heads have no qualification and less than 3 per cent have a technical qualification.

'Capabilities' have been interpreted in this specific urban marginalization context as functionings or achieved outcomes, and not as mere opportunities people have to be adequately sheltered, to live a healthy life, to be educated and work, should they choose it or not. Given the local context, it is very unlikely that the fact that adolescents in the *villas* do not complete secondary education, or that young people are neither at work nor at school, is the result of personal choice rather than lack of opportunities. As Wolff and De-Shalit (2013) have argued in the case of the low health achievements of the inhabitants of inner city Glasgow, even if they have the same opportunities to live a healthy life than others, in the sense of having the same access to the National Health Service, their poor health achievements has more to do with unemployment carried over through generations than lifestyle choices.

The above statistics also reveal that capability deprivations reinforce each other. The inability to achieve one set of being and doing leads to an

TABLE 4.4 Indicators of the capability to work in Buenos Aires

	Buenos Aires	Non-villas	Villas
Percentage of young people (aged 18–24) unemployed	26.6	26.3	31.2
Percentage of unemployed household heads	11.3	10.9	24.5
Percentage of female unemployment	17.0	16.0	34.0
Percentage of employed population in the formal sector	57.4	58.6	21.3
Percentage of employed population in industry	10.4	10.3	14.4
Percentage of employed population in construction	3.3	2.7	20.5
Percentage of employed population in shops and restaurants	20.6	20.3	29.8
Percentage of employed population in economic services	25.5	25.9	12.5
Percentage of employed population in social services	34.0	34.7	11.4
Percentage of employed population in domestic services	5.1	4.9	11.2
Percentage of household heads with professional qualifications	25.2	25.9	0.9
Percentage of household heads with technical qualifications	23.7	24.2	2.6
Percentage of household heads without qualification	15.2	14.4	46.1

Source: Macció and Lépore (2012), on the basis of 2010 national census and 2009 household survey

inability to achieve another set of being and doing, what Wolff and De-Shalit (2007) have coined 'corrosive capability'. The very fact of living in a *villa*, and how one fares in 'being adequately sheltered', affects how one fares in the doing of 'working', in the being of 'living a long and healthy life', in the 'being educated and equipped with the necessary qualifications to engage in meaningful work'. On the basis of a multidimensional poverty index,[6] which includes ten indicators in the dimensions of housing, health and subsistence, Macció and Lépore (2012: 84–102) have calculated that the single determining factor for being multi-dimensionally poor (that is, deprived in at least one dimension) was living in the *villas*. While families with a household head with complete secondary education were less likely to be multi-dimensionally poor outside the *villas*, the level of education of household heads had virtually no effect on whether families in the *villas* were multi-dimensionally poor or not.

Moving beyond national household survey data, using the language of the capability approach to assess what type of lives people succeed in living will also involve collecting specific data about other valuable sets of beings and doings that the capability literature has highlighted. Nussbaum's list has been the most widespread reference in that matter. As the purpose of this chapter is not to assess per se the lives of people in the *villas* but to show how to use the capability approach to that effect, it will limit itself to mentioning some relevant capabilities about which it would be worthwhile to get data.

Given the high number of children per family in the *villas*, having access to reproductive health, captured by data about the contraceptive prevalence rate, would be an additional valuable capability to include in the assessment.[7] Another central human capability which Nussbaum has singled out is that of 'being able to be secure against assault, including sexual assault, child sexual abuse, and domestic violence' as part of her capability for bodily integrity. How widespread is domestic violence? How widespread are criminal assaults? A survey among 480 families in two *villas* reported that more than half of the people interviewed had been a victim, or a member of their family had been a victim, of theft in the previous year (Lépore 2012: 225). Data from the Argentinian Supreme Court of Justice showed that, in 2010, the *villas* had a homicide rate of 12.7 per 100,000 inhabitants, compared to 3.08 for the rest of the city of Buenos Aires.[8]

As part of her 'capability for affiliation', Nussbaum mentions 'having the social bases of self-respect and non-humiliation' as a valuable functioning. Are people treated differently by public services or by employers because they live in a *villa*? There are no official statistics on this but the above-mentioned study in two *villas* reported that 35 per cent of the people interviewed had felt discriminated against because of where they lived (Lépore 2012: 256). This relatively low level of subjective sense of discrimination may be due to the fact that not many inhabitants often go outside the *villas* and therefore are not aware of the severe lack of opportunities they have compared to other parts of the city. They may also have internalized the structural discrimination and no longer see it. Discrimination becomes part of normal life. The study led by Mitchell (2012) reported that many residents worked mainly in the *villas* and shopped there too. Some civil society organizations did, however, try to broaden the horizons of residents, by bringing in volunteers and professionals from outside and taking children on outings so that they can interact with the rest of society.

Another valuable capability worth mentioning is the capability to enjoy aesthetic experience and/or relate to the natural environment.[9] To what extent do the inhabitants of the *villas* have the opportunities to access spaces of beauty and nature? What is the proportion of parks and green spaces in the *villas* compared to the rest of the city? Collecting data on these would be highly relevant for the assessment of the social reality. However, creating such spaces has to be seen within the wider context of exclusion. In one *villa* of greater Buenos Aires, there was a joint initiative by the local government and rubbish collecting company to build a park, which contained a football field, a children's playground and trees and flowers. This may count in the data as one green and recreation space. But the park soon became the rallying point for drug addicts and it became too dangerous for children to play there and for people to enjoy the space. Municipal workers refused to maintain the plants and flowers because of fear of aggression. The park is now abandoned and all but green, peaceful and recreational.[10]

A valuable capability often mentioned by Sen among the ones that 'people have reason to choose and value' is the capability to participate in the life of the community. How do people in the *villas* fare in this capability? In a study of civil society organizations active in two *villas*, Bajo Flores and Barracas, conducted between December 2010 and August 2011, Mitchell (2012: 127) reported that there was one organization for 503 people in Barracas, and that 64 per cent of the population participated or benefited from them. In Bajo Flores, there was one organization for 604 people and 46 per cent of the population participated in them.[11] A survey among 480 households in the two *villas* found similar results of relatively high levels of participation. Approximately 44 per cent of the families interviewed said they participated in at least one organization (Lépore 2012: 235). The organizations with the largest outreach are those associated with the Catholic parishes. In Barracas, one in five residents participate in at least one organization of the parish, which includes a popular kitchen, a drug rehabilitation centre, a home for young and elderly people, a youth centre, a secondary school, a professional training centre, a legal services centre and a sports centre, among others.

As for political participation, achievements are very low. Only 15 per cent of the 13,500 people registered for voting voted in the 2008 local elections of the *Junta Vecinal* de Bajo Flores (Mitchell 2012: 175), an organization which is supposed to represent the inhabitants of the *villas* among state authorities. A fifth of the people interviewed in the two *villas* did not even know that a *Junta de Vecinos* representing their interests existed. Participation in political parties is also very low. Only 1 per cent of the people interviewed said that they were affiliated to a political organization (Lépore 2012: 236). This political apathy and indifference may be due in part to the large number of undocumented persons who live in the *villas*, and therefore have no voting rights, and to the fact that one is discriminated against if one does not belong to the ruling party.

As for the capabilities which people themselves 'have reason to choose and value', two capabilities stood out from the interviews conducted by Lépore *et al.* (2012): the capability to live in a drug-free, peaceful and secure environment, and to live in decent housing in a normal urban area. The four issues that the people interviewed were the most dissatisfied with were:

public transport, work, housing and security, with security receiving the highest dissatisfaction rating, followed by inappropriate housing conditions (problems of damp, cold and overcrowding) and lack of urbanization, with taxis and ambulances not entering the streets of the *villas* and an irregular bus service (Lépore 2012: 220–3). A survey of civil society organizations yielded the same results as the top priority areas of the *villas*: drugs, housing and violence (Mitchell 2012: 147). Although 60 per cent of the organizations mentioned drug addiction as a problem, only 11 per cent of all organizations were dealing with it, either at prevention level through offering alternative activities for young people, or at rehabilitation level. Although more than half of the organizations interviewed reported housing as a problem, only three organizations dealt with housing. Insecurity was cited by half of the organizations as a problem but there is no organization which deals with insecurity, violence and crime – this large discrepancy between what is diagnosed as a problem and what is being done about it will be discussed below. The majority of civil society organizations active in the *villas* are dealing with food, education and social work.

Transforming unjust structures

The two capabilities that residents value most, namely living in a drug-free and peaceful environment and living in a normal urban area, move the assessment in a structural direction, for it belongs to no individual inhabitant as such to be free of drug-related violence or to be treated with respect as a full citizen of the city. This capability is relational. It depends on how people relate to each other both at the interpersonal and structural level. What is the quality of economic, social and political structures in the *villas* and more widely in the city of Buenos Aires and Argentina? Do they provide the structuring conditions for people to live well in a shared space? The remainder of this section will not engage in a detailed analysis of the situation of Argentina but give some pointers for how to conduct such an analysis and emphasize how structures are built, reproduced or transformed through people's agency.

Starting with economic relations, most people in the *villas* work in the informal sector and do not have access to adequate social protection. An analysis of the quality of the economic structure would require an investigation of the reasons for which the share of the informal economy as part of the overall Argentinian economy grew and which specific economic policy decisions taken by specific actors contributed to the informalization of the economy. Other useful information for analysing the quality of the economic structure relates to macro-economic stability. Of particular concern is the inflation rate which official government statistics grossly under-estimate.[12] This has considerable effects on the ability that people have to buy basic commodities and achieve a set of basic capabilities such as being adequately nourished and sheltered. Information about the government's monetary policy would be useful in this regard. The macro-economic and labour structures are not given but are created by the deliberate actions of economic actors through, among others, public spending and fiscal and monetary policy. Other decisions which have accounted for the growth of the *villas* and the above capability deprivation are the government's economic policies, especially the macro-economic mismanagement and exchange rate policies which led to the 2001–2 economic crisis and the policies of labour flexibilization in the 1990s which led to the growing informalization of labour markets.[13]

At the social level, relations between people in the *villas* are characterized by a limited sense of social cohesion and perception of common collective identity. This is due in part to the large migration from other countries, which is not conducive to generating a sense of unity to trigger strong political participation (Lépore 2012: 206),[14] and in part to the significant levels of violence, which limit people's freedom of movement. In that respect, civil society organizations play an important role in providing a space for sociability safe from violence (Mitchell 2012: 160), but their scope for transforming social relations at a structural level and reducing segregation between those who live inside and outside the *villas*, is limited.

Addressing violence and the lack of urbanization not only requires local organizations dealing with addiction and housing problems but it also requires a state response. That the social structure is characterized by con-flict and discrimination is not an accident but the result of policy decisions taken, or not taken. The Argentinian government currently has no proper drug policy regarding one of the most prevalent and devastating drugs in the *villas*, paco.[15] It is part of a wider addiction policy and has yet to be criminalized. Some social movements, such as Mothers against Paco, are trying to change government policy and make the sale and use of paco illegal, but they face political structures which are not open to incorporating their demands.[16]

That economic and social structures are not conducive to people having opportunities to do or be what they have reason to value has its fundamental root in political structures being diverted from the end of establishing the conditions for people's wellbeing, and more precisely, in the failure of political actors to act justly. As a resident of the *villa* of Barracas expressed it, 'The problem of the *villas* is a political problem. There is no political will to solve the problem. Meanwhile, they [the government] give us the scraps

[targeted social assistance programmes in food, health and education]'
(Mitchell 2012: 168).

The drug, violence, housing and work problems in the *villas* are not only
the result of government actors failing to act towards providing the
conditions for every person to enjoy a set of valuable capabilities, it is also,
and arguably foremost, the result of the inhabitants of the *villas* themselves
failing to act collectively, as a group, towards that aim. In other words, it is
a failure of collective agency. The extremely low rate of political participation was already highlighted above. There is de facto no political organization representative of the *villas* in front of government authorities. This
makes joint decisions on urban planning difficult. The one that exists, the
Junta de Vecinos, has very low support among the population.

When there is engagement with political structures, and when action
does occur to press the government to respond to people's claims, it is
usually targeted at gaining specific resources and dealt with in a personalized
manner. Mitchell (2012: 174) reports of an interviewee talking directly to
leaders of the state organization responsible for providing public services in
the *villas* to solve problems of electricity cuts, and another one talking
directly to the ministry of education to demand that his cooperative business
gets the contract for cleaning a state school which just opened in exchange
for a percentage of the contract going to the minister. These actions are not
likely to have a strong impact on changing public service delivery and
employment policies. They are creating further social and political frag-
mentation and are perpetuating a political structure characterized by a lack
of transparency and by corruption – as Chapter 3 has argued, the reality of
structural injustice does not detract from individual responsibility in perpetuating the injustice.

From the above analysis of the *villas* of Buenos Aires using the language
of the capability approach, one can conclude that remedying the injustice
that its inhabitants suffer critically relies on the extent and nature of their
political representation to establish the conditions for their wellbeing. The
villas miseria are not a natural phenomenon. They are the result of human-
made decisions, and can be transformed through human agency. Which type
of political action would be the most appropriate is for the people themselves
to decide. The broad-based organizing which transformed the slums of
Chicago in the 1930s provided the inspiration for London citizens and the
transformation of inner city London in the 2000s.[17] The wellbeing of the
people of the *villas* of Buenos Aires depends on their agency. The language
of the capability approach gives no blueprint to act. Each context must yield
its own responses, as the next section goes on to discuss.

The smelter town of La Oroya, Peru

La Oroya is a town of 18,600 inhabitants (according to the 2007 census), 185 km north-east of Lima, at 3,750 m above sea level in the Central Andes of Peru, and at a crossing point on the Central Highway, connecting Lima with the Andes and the rain forest. The visitor is immediately struck by the lack of vegetation, the thick grey cap which hovers constantly over the mountains and the river in which no fish can be seen (Valencia 2012a: 13). The metallurgic industry has been dominating the town since the 1920s when the American company Cerro de Pasco built a smelter to process the metals which were being mined in the surrounding areas. It was nationalized in the early 1970s as Centromin Peru, and sold in the late 1990s to the American company Doe Run. The smelter is the main source of employment of the town. In 2009, more than 4,000 inhabitants directly or indirectly depended on the smelter for their living. But the smelter is also the main source of pollution. In 2006, the Blacksmith Institute, an independent environmental action group, nominated La Oroya as one of the ten most polluted cities in the world.[18] The inhabitants of La Oroya may earn a living, but this has come at the cost of their health (Valencia 2012a, b).

The kinds of lives people are living

As with the reality of urban marginalization in Argentina, analysing the reality of La Oroya with the language of the capability approach starts with the question: 'What kind of lives are people able to live? Are they able to be or do what they have reason to value?' A 2001 socio-economic study of La Oroya reported the following data: 35.1 per cent of the population was under 15 years of age, 37 per cent were migrants from other parts of Peru, 83.7 per cent of households had a male breadwinner, women only composed 3 per cent of the economically active population, 33.4 per cent of households contributed to a public health-care system and 3.4 per cent to private health care, leaving 43 per cent without access to health protection. There were problems of alcoholism in 42.4 per cent of the households, nearly one out of four households had problems of domestic violence, and one out of ten had problems of drug addiction (Valencia 2012a: 156–7). About 25 per cent of the inhabitants worked directly in the smelter and they received on average salaries twice or three times higher than the rest of the town (Valencia 2012a: 189). The most recent socio-demographic data are from the 2007 National Census, and further affirm the limited opportunities that the inhabitants of La Oroya have to live a healthy life, for only half of them have access to health care,[19] which is a concern given the health damage caused by environmental contamination.

According to a study made by a civil society organization, there were only five breathable days in 2006 and only one in 2007, if one considered the standards set by the World Health Organization for what accounts as breathable air without threatening human health (Valencia 2012a: 26). According to studies summarized in the Report on La Oroya by the International Federation of Human Rights:[20] between 1998 and 2009, the levels of sulphur dioxide in the atmosphere were frequently above the maximum level allowed by Peruvian environmental standards; in 2002, 80 per cent of children had blood levels two or three times higher than the maximum limit allowed by the World Health Organization; in 2005, urine tests on the population of La Oroya revealed that those living in the old city where the smelter was located had significantly higher levels of contamination than those living further away; all newborn babies in La Oroya had lead in their blood and 25 per cent of them already had lead levels beyond the limit set by the World Health Organization. A study conducted by three civil society organizations of the dust contained in the floor of 35 houses, one school and three shops in La Oroya found that 88 per cent of the 50 dust samples taken had levels of lead higher than the US standard for safety, and 100 per cent of the samples taken from the old city had levels dangerous to health.[21]

Despite these high levels of lead, cadmium, arsenic and other toxic substances found in the city, and given the scientific evidence of the impact of high lead levels on brain and neurological development and tissue growth, no epidemiological study linking these to ill-health incidence in La Oroya has been carried out (Valencia 2012a: 247–8). There are no official data on cancer rates or learning difficulties among children, although children report lack of concentration and suffering from aching bones and people talk of cancer deaths.[22]

In June 2009, smelter activities were suspended as a result of a bankruptcy procedure and air pollution level was noted to have sharply decreased, but as soon as activities partially resumed in July 2012, pollution noticeably increased.[23] Notwithstanding cleaner air today, whatever pollution control measures or cleaning operations are enforced now, the damage caused by lead and other toxics on health are irreversible.

Translated into capability language, the above data are indicators of how few opportunities the inhabitants of La Oroya have to live in a non-polluted environment and to live a healthy life. They face a trade-off between working in the town and enduring the risk of suffering ill health or migrating to an uncertain future elsewhere, with the likelihood of economic and social opportunities losses. They may have opportunities for employment, but their opportunity set is limited to working in the smelter

or working in a polluted environment. Working in the smelter also gives them housing benefits and health insurance. This further compounds their socio-economic dependence on the employer who damages their health.

If one were to enrich available data with a set of predetermined valuable capabilities, such as Nussbaum's list, one could add some data about the capability to express emotions. Many people who have mobilized to press the Peruvian state and smelter to comply with environmental regulation live in fear. One lady who owned a restaurant where smelter workers used to come to have lunch lost all her clientele when she started to campaign for a clean La Oroya. She had to stop her environmental activism out of fear. Other environmental campaigners have been physically abused and many threatened (Valencia 2012a: 207). This lack of capability to express one's emotions and suffering severely affects the capability for voice and political participation, which is so central to Sen's thinking.

From her fieldwork conducted between September and December 2010, Valencia (2012a) tells stories of people fearing to express their pain and stories of deep divisions with regard to the perception itself of suffering. The inhabitants of La Oroya were divided between those who voiced their pain of having their jobs at risk – the company threatened to close down the smelter if it had to comply with environmental regulation by agreed deadlines – and those who voiced their pain of witnessing the ecosystem of the region being destroyed and their health being at risk. In this context of division about what aches most, losing one's job or losing one's health, a context heightened by the manipulation and power exercised by the company to divide the local community,[24] it is very difficult for united action to take place in order to force the company, and the Peruvian state, to comply with their legal obligations.

As in the above analysis of the slums of Buenos Aires, the concepts of capability and functioning overlap. No one would choose, should one have the opportunity of not doing so, to live in a polluted environment and suffer ill health for the sake of it. The ill health may well be the consequence of the choice of living in La Oroya or working in the smelter – people could go and live or work elsewhere – but to what extent is it a genuine choice? Should similar socio-economic opportunities be offered in a clean environment, would people still choose to work in a polluted one? Moreover, some have lived in La Oroya for generations and are resisting a move elsewhere because of attachment to the land of their forbearers. If they want to protect their health, the options are migrating to an uncertain future or mobilizing to make the state regulate the smelter company and make the company compliant. But the facts that economic security is generally more valued than economic insecurity, and that the company intimidated those who

between those who campaigned to protect their jobs and those who campaigned to protect their health. This division was compounded by the company threatening with dismissal anyone questioning, or associating with someone questioning, its compliance with environmental regulation.[30]

Political relations are not that of equal citizens having equal access to the state. The Peruvian state has been grossly privileging the smelter company above people's wellbeing. This started as early as the beginning of last century when the state was helping the US-based Cerro de Pasco Corporation to transform economic relations in the region into bonded labour and has continued ever since to prioritize economic benefits over the wellbeing of the population. It continued when the smelter was nationalized under Centromin Peru and was reinforced under the ownership of Doe Run when the smelter was privatized in 1997. The saga regarding the implementation of an environmental mitigation plan, which was agreed at the time of privatization of the smelter in 1997, is a highly relevant symptom of how political relations in La Oroya, and beyond, are characterized.

A condition of the privatization sale in 1997 was the completion by 2007 of an environmental mitigation plan. During the 1990s, environmental social movements acquired more power in the national political scene and pressed the Peruvian government to introduce its first environmental regulations laws. The environmental mitigation plan held the Peruvian state responsible for cleaning up the soil pollution, and Doe Run for treating water, disposing properly of solid waste, and controlling and treating its toxic gas emissions (Valencia 2012a: 16). Doe Run procrastinated in its environmental regulation compliance and asked for a three-year extension of the plan on the ground that economic hardship prevented them from investing in the technology required to process the toxic wastes. The Peruvian state then declared that it would not start its cleaning up operations until Doe Run started to act, as it was felt that there was no point in cleaning up the soil while air pollution continued. Doe Run threatened to close the smelter and lay off staff if this extension was not granted. The deadline for completion was therefore extended to October 2009 (Valencia 2012a: 20). As the extended deadline was approaching, Doe Run asked for a second extension until April 2011, but in June 2009 it filed for bankruptcy and suspended its activities. According to information from the Report by the International Federation of Human Rights on La Oroya, the bankruptcy was the result of a fraud and Ira Rennert, the billionaire owner of Doe Run, is now being prosecuted in Peruvian courts for submitting a fictive insolvency.[31] To date, the Peruvian state is yet to clean up soil pollution, and Doe Run has only built two acid plants to treat its lead and zinc smelter emissions. As noted above, air contamination rates increased as an immediate effect of the smelter's resumption of activities and there is no cleaning up operation in the pipeline. The Peruvian government passed a law in 2008 that the maximum limit of sulphuric emissions of 80ug/m^3 would decrease to 20ug/m^3 on 1 January 2014. However, in July 2013, the government announced that it would exempt companies from the law if they could demonstrate that no technology exists to filter the emissions. Three cities, among which is La Oroya, are exempted from the law.[32] This is another illustration of the power that corporations have in Peru to shift environmental laws to suit their economic interests.

The political reality at the micro-level in La Oroya echoes that at the national level. When a special Ministry of the Environment was created in Peru in 2008, metal mining and hydrocarbons were excluded from its terms of reference (Thorp 2012: 123). All companies in the extractive sector have, since 1992, been required by law to provide an environmental impact assessment, but Thorp (2012: 123) notes that the Ministry of Energy and Mines has yet to reject a business investment proposal on the basis of its environmental impact assessment. This is, in fact, not surprising given that all environmental impact assessments have to be approved by the Ministry of Energy and Mines, and not the Ministry of the Environment, to acquire legitimacy.[33] According to the government Ombudsman, the Defensora del Pueblo, there were 154 cases of socio-environmental conflicts in Peru in April 2013, with 112 cases directly related to mining activities and 20 cases to hydrocarbons.[34]

Despite their current poor quality and poor orientation to building the conditions for people to live in a clean environment and be healthy, political structures remain the ones offering the space of action to build such conditions. Paradoxically, political structures undermine the conditions for people to live well but they also uniquely offer a channel for these conditions to be restored. Businesses, and especially mining ones, may have a greater access to the state but other social actors do have access to the state too. Environmental groups have managed to make their voices heard and press the elected members of parliament to introduce new environmental laws. Organizations like the Defensora del Pueblo, the Observatory for Mining Conflicts, the Confederación Nacional de Comunidades del Perú Afectadas por la Minería (CONACAMI) and the Asociación Interétnica de Desarrollo de la Selva Peruana (AIDESEP) do play an important role in voicing the concerns of those whose land and lives are affected by mining.[35] The public reasoning process in Peru may not yet be characterized by the ability of actors to engage with other people's perspectives, but the more people who suffer are able to express their pain, the more it is likely that they will be heard and a dialogue can start about what causes their suffering and how this could be remedied. At the local level, the Movement for Health for La Oroya, a social movement gathering various community, human rights, non-governmental and church organizations, was very influential in voicing the suffering of the people hurt by the smelter, as the next chapter will detail.

Peru still has an independent judiciary. This allows people who suffer from environmental degradation to sue the state for not fulfilling its obligations. They also have access to international political structures such as the Inter-American Commission on Human Rights which can further pressure the Peruvian state to comply with international human rights conventions. Given that the company who is responsible for human rights abuse in La Oroya is registered in the US, American political structures are also a channel to transform the quality of political relations in Peru. Exposure of Doe Run's abuses in the American media, and exposure of child health violation by a Doe Run subsidiary in Missouri, helped bring the case into the US. American civil society organizations can then apply political pressure for Doe Run to stop destroying people's health and the environment, and for the Peruvian state to stop being complicit in this destruction.

Like the situation of exclusion and segregation of Buenos Aires, the situation of La Oroya is not a natural accident, it is the result of the agency of social actors taken at different moments in time. It is only through their agency that the situation can be transformed. The Peruvian state and mining businesses are acting within a specific epistemological structure which associates development with higher economic incomes and which assumes that people's lives will automatically be improved as a consequence of a rise in economic output. Social actors can change this epistemological structure, which justifies the destruction of the environment and the losses of livelihoods of a minority for the sake of greater wellbeing for the majority.[36] The normative language of the capability approach precisely challenges such epistemological structure by offering an alternative evaluation framework to assess what constitutes wellbeing. The consumption of more metal-based goods in one part of the world often entails a loss of opportunities for people in another part of the world to achieve a set of certain valuable beings and doings, such as living a life in harmony with the natural environment. The language frames the problem differently from the way the economic utilitarian language frames it.

Beyond the manual guide

This chapter has attempted to offer some guidelines for using the normative language of the capability approach to assess situations and transform them so as to make them less unjust. It is far from being a manual guide or toolkit. When one learns a new language, its keywords and basic grammar have to be learned and assimilated in order to speak it. But once this is done, the speaker has millions of ways of using these words in the specific situations in which he or she finds him- or herself. Similarly, the basic words and grammar of the capability approach have to be well understood and internalized, but how to use the normative language is left open given that it depends on the situation in which a judgement has to be made and an action to be taken. There are myriad ways in which the capability approach can be used, from designing new internationally comparable multidimensional measures of poverty (Alkire and Santos 2013), to constructing new higher education pedagogies (Boni and Walker 2013), to evaluating the reach of 'corporate social responsibility' in making companies responsible towards society and the environment (Lompo and Trani 2013).

As has been emphasized throughout the book, there is no unique use of the capability approach, but instead there are multiple uses. An economist may have focused specifically on doing a household survey to create new capability-related indicators, an educationalist on assessing the pedagogies and curriculum of the schools from a capability perspective, and a political scientist on assessing the political capabilities of people. This chapter has proposed an analysis from a certain interpretation of Amartya Sen's works on wellbeing, development and justice and their inter-linkages.

As a normative language, the capability approach is not learned only in books but also through practice. As no language can be learned without others, the capability approach similarly needs groups of people already attempting to practise it. The next, and final, chapter discusses the making of this new normative language.

Notes

1 Sen (1992: 49) talks of this shift of the evaluation space from utility to capabilities as having a 'good deal of discriminating power, both because of what it *includes* as potentially valuable and because of what it *excludes* from the list of objects to be weighted as intrinsically important'.

2 UN-Habitat estimates that 863 million people lived in slums in 2012, compared to 650 million in 1990 and 760 million in 2000. See the April 2013 UN-Habitat Brochure 'Time to Think Urban' (p. 15) at http://www.unhabitat.org/pmss/listItemDetails.aspx?publicationID=3456.

3 According to the International Council on Mining and Minerals, the value of global minerals production was globally four times higher in 2010 than in 2002, and more countries had acquired an economic dependence on mineral exports. See the report 'The Role of Mining in National Economies' at http://www.icmm.com/the-role-of-mining-in-national-economies. In Latin America, socio-environmental conflicts have been growing steadily in the last decade. The Observatory of Mining Conflicts in Latin America counted 189 such conflicts in 2012, see http://basedatos.conflictosmineros.net/ocmal_db.

4 For a discussion of the 'Washington Consensus' policies, see Gore (2000) and Naim (2000).

5 On the basis of national census data, Macció and Lépore (2012: 52–3) estimated that the population of the *villas* grew from 52,000 people in 1991 to 165,000 in 2010. In relative terms, as a percentage of total population of the city, this represents an increase from 1.8 per cent in 1991 to 5.7 per cent in 2010. The real figure may be higher, however, given illegal immigration from neighbouring countries.

6 See Alkire and Santos (2013) for the methodology of computing multi-dimensional poverty indices. See also publications of the team of the Oxford Poverty and Human Development Initiative at www.ophi.org.uk.

7 From interviews conducted in two *villas*, it was found that women had widespread access to contraception but that, in the absence of other opportunities, being a mother was often the only life project readily accessible to young women in the *villas* (Ann Mitchell, personal communication).

8 See http://www.csjn.gov.ar/dbei/ii/ii.html.

9 Alkire (2002) included aesthetic experience and peace of mind as valuable dimensions of wellbeing.

10 I thank Augusto Zampini for this example.

11 Mitchell (2012: 123) divided civil society organizations into grassroots organizations created by the people of the community themselves (such as community centres, popular kitchens, neighbourhood associations) and external organizations founded outside the community (such as religious and human rights organizations).

12 The government puts the inflation rate officially at 10 per cent but trade unions estimate it at 25–30 per cent. See http://blogs.elpais.com/el-sur/2013/04/de-como-el-ministro-argentino-de-economia-combate-la-inflacion.html

13 For an analysis of economic policy in Argentina over the last 30 years, see Cruces and Gasparini (2009).

14 Among the 480 families interviewed in Bajo Flores and Barracas, 20 per cent of household heads were from Buenos Aires, 27 per cent were internal Argentinian migrants, 25 per cent were Bolivians, 22 per cent Paraguayans and 5 per cent Peruvians and others (Lépore 2012: 219).

15 Paco is a chemical residue of the fabrication of cocaine and is relatively cheap (1 gram sells for 1 peso), but its addiction effects are immediate and there is irreversible brain damage after six months of use. See http://www.lanacion.com.ar/822406-crecio-200-el-consumo-de-paco.

16 See http://www.madrescontraelpaco.org.ar. According to an article dated February 2011, the mother who started the movement said that, when she met with President Cristina Kirchner, the meeting was more about publicity and political campaigning for her party than concern for the mothers who lost their children to paco. See http://www.argentinaindependent.com/feature/paco-drug-epidemic-sweeping-the-streets-of-argentina.

17 See http://www.citizensuk.org.
18 See http://www.blacksmithinstitute.org/the-2006-top-ten-of-worst-polluted-places.html.
19 See Instituto Nacional de Estadística e Informática. Censos Nacionales 2007: XI de Población y VI de Vivienda, available at http://desa.inei.gob.pe/censos 2007/tabulados/.
20 International Federation of Human Rights (FIDH), 'Metallurgical Complex of La Oroya: When investor protection threatens human rights', at http://www.fidh.org/IMG/pdf/metallurgical_complex_of_la_oroya-2.pdf. The report was released on 7 May 2013.
21 The study 'Interior Dust Lead Levels in La Oroya' conducted by Cornejo and Gottesfeld is available at http://www.spda.org.pe:8081/archivo_digital/bit stream/handle/123456789/21/Interior%20Dust.pdf?sequence=1.
22 See the video 'House of Lead: A Story of Greed' at http://www.youtube.com/watch?v=Kpwu8DOmzoU.
23 The smelter reopened on 28 July 2012, and between 1 and 24 August, the levels of sulphur dioxide already exceeded the upper permissible limit during 10 days (Report of the FIDH, p. 15).
24 A person interviewed by Valencia (2012a: 207) recounts the story of a Christmas gathering where all the children of La Oroya were supposed to receive toys donated by Doe Run. The company systematically refused to give toys to the children whose parents were among the environmental campaigners.
25 The next chapter will discuss this in greater detail when analysing the dynamics of agency in the case of the Movement for Health of La Oroya.
26 A local inhabitant reported that he had been making a living out of fishing trout in the river but from 1953 onwards, the fish died and he was forced to find employment at the smelter. Another recalled her aunt saying that the feet of the chicken and sheep were burned and animals then died (Valencia 2012a: 177–8).
27 Scurrah et al. (2009: 167) note that this 1901 law enabled Cerro de Pasco to buy 80 per cent of all the mines in the Central Highlands and to acquire a monopoly on smelter activities. In the 1920s, the company controlled 32 per cent of the whole of Peru's exports, thus yielding significant economic and political influence.
28 See 'Tercer informe cartográfico sobre las concesiones mineras en el Peru sobre base de datos de Junio 2012' at http://www.cooperaccion.org.pe/images/pdf/JUNIO2012/situacion.pdf.
29 For details of how social and economic relations are intermingled in Peru and how inequality at the economic, social and political levels reinforces each other, see Thorp and Paredes (2010).
30 The Ministry of Work did offer smelter workers retraining opportunities to work elsewhere, but workers refused because the majority of them were aged above 50 and many did not even have a complete secondary education. No other option would have given them the same socio-economic benefits (Valencia 2012b: 13).
31 At the same time, Ira Rennert is suing the Peruvian state for discrimination and for not following the Free Trade Treaty between the US and Peru, and is asking for compensation of US$800 million from the state (Report of the FIDH, pp. 19–20).
32 See http://elcomercio.pe/actualidad/1608150/noticia-editorial-parche-ambiental; http://elcomercio.pe/economia/1602210/noticia-fundiciones-ilo-oroya-no-dejaran-operar-2014.
33 Personal communication from Areli Valencia.

34 See http://www.defensoria.gob.pe/modules/Downloads/conflictos/2013/
Reporte-Mensual-conflictos-Sociales-110-Abril-2013.pdf.

35 However, organizations representative of those living in the Andes and Amazon
remain politically discriminated against, and discussions deeply polarized (personal
communication from Andrea Baertl).

36 The previous president of Peru, Alan Garcia, said in relation to people protesting
against the dispossession of their land that: 'These people are not first class citizens.
Four hundred thousand native people cannot tell us, we the twenty eight millions
of Peruvians: you have no right to come here' (available on YouTube 'Alan
Garcia y los ciudadanos de primera clase').

5

THE FORMING AND
SPEAKING OF THE LANGUAGE

The capability approach without copyrights

How can this language for assessing and transforming situations from the
perspective of wellbeing and agency be acquired? How to bring concerns
for how well people live in a shared natural environment to the centre of
human decisions and actions? A language is not learned only through reading about its vocabulary and grammar but foremost through practice by
engaging in social relationships. Anyone who knows a language other than
his or her mother tongue is very acutely aware that without practice, a
language can quickly be forgotten. Languages die without being sustained
by social relationships, this is also the case with the normative language of
the capability approach and its perspective of human freedom.

This chapter examines how a language, which has wellbeing and agency
at its core, can be learned and spoken. It discusses the critical role of groups
and relationships in forming agency, in nurturing people's ability to act so
that oneself, and others, have opportunities to do or be what they have
reason to value. But before doing so, it starts with developing an argument
already alluded to earlier, that the capability approach does not have copyright on its keywords of agency and wellbeing.

Amartya Sen presented a moral approach from the perspective of freedom
which is fundamentally open-ended, incomplete and ambiguous. It can be
interpreted in various ways according to the situation the social analyst has
to address. This section continues this line of argument by showing how the
capability approach is versatile not only in accommodating elements from
various, and even apparently competing, normative frameworks, but also in

being incorporated into them and so enabling mutual enrichment. This section focuses on feminist, environmental and religious normative frameworks.

Martha Nussbaum is undoubtedly the scholar who has worked the most at making the capability approach a form of feminist political theory. The elaboration of her list of central human capabilities was born from the experience of the suffering and marginalization of women who too often are told by dominating men what is a valuable set of doing and being and what is not, in order to maintain their position of control and domination. Nussbaum has built an interpretation of the capability approach in relation to a feminist reading of Rawls's political liberalism. She has kept one of the main features of liberal feminist political theory, namely that justice for women lies in the granting of the freedom to pursue a life of their own choosing,[1] but has argued for central human capabilities rather than primary goods to be the object of distributive justice. States have the responsibility to provide opportunities for all women, and men, to enjoy a set of central human capabilities so that they each can live a life of their own choice, and not be forced into a life dictated by social norms or economic circumstances. Obviously, this remains an ever unattainable ideal for many, but nonetheless, Nussbaum's capabilities approach offers an analytical framework to assess whether women's lives are indeed women's own chosen lives or whether their lives are owned by a patriarchal social order or exploitative economic system, and by doing so, it aims at guiding social and political action to free women's lives from domination and exploitation.

Like other feminist theorists, Nussbaum attributes a central role to the family in shaping relationships of equality or domination, for it is in the family that patriarchal norms are formed.[2] In this regard, the capability approach borrows from radical forms of feminist theories, which argue that equal rights for men and women are not sufficient, for these rights are implemented within the context of a patriarchal social order. To give an example taken from Bryson (2003: 197), a law may give women the right to leave an abusive husband but such law is not sufficient to protect women from domestic violence. If women have nowhere to go – their families may not take their daughter back and may force her to stay within her marriage, or women may not find opportunities for employment to be economically independent, or there are no organizations helping women suffering from domestic violence – the law is of little help in advancing justice for women and enabling them to enjoy central human capabilities.

The capability approach, or rather the capabilities approach as Nussbaum calls her interpretation, incorporates elements from radical feminist political theories, with their focus on liberation from a patriarchal social order,[3] by emphasizing that the inequality of gender power relations needs to be addressed and that women's bodies need to be liberated from men's control if women are to be given opportunities to live a life of their own choosing. In this sense, the capabilities approach links radical and liberal forms of feminisms. It recognizes the centrality of patriarchy in depriving women of opportunities to live a life they have reason to choose and value, while it emphasizes at the same time the centrality of each woman's life and of public reasoning processes to liberate women from patriarchy.

In addition to embracing in fruitful tension the reasoning and individual focus of liberal feminism and the revolutionary and collective focus of radical feminism, it also embraces in fruitful tension the views of 'each person as an end' (Nussbaum 2000: 69) and of the intrinsic sociality of human life. A major feminist concern is that, far too often, women's lives have been sacrificed for the sake of a group's or men's interests, and that therefore ethical individualism is best for women (Robeyns 2008). It is indeed critical, if one is concerned about women's lives, to look at how well each woman's life is doing individually and not how well her family or clan or community is doing. Nonetheless, the capability approach is equally concerned with recognizing that women's lives, like any human life, are also constituted by complex relationships. Assessing how well a woman is, is therefore inseparable from these relationships (see Chapter 2). What a feminist may perceive as an abusive relationship, the woman in that relationship may perceive as security. In a study of Afghan women's wellbeing, Trani et al. (2011) have shown that honouring one's community is a major component of how women valued a life well lived. Such honouring may entail that women are deprived of educational opportunities but Trani et al. warn that one must be very cautious in dismissing the importance of family or clan honour. The wellbeing of each woman is better served through working at her liberation from oppression from within these relationships, even if they are initially abusive, and transforming them rather than simply rejecting them for being oppressive and depriving them of other valuable beings and doings.[4]

Environmental ethics is another area where the capability approach happily embraces what may appear as contrasting viewpoints. As with feminism, the capability approach encompasses both elements from liberal and critical theory when it comes to dealing with environmental justice (Schlosberg 2009). It is not only concerned with what distribution of goods should be (liberal theory) but also with the processes behind a maldistribution of goods (critical theory). The capability approach assesses the distribution of goods according to the extent to which it enables each person to function well but it also examines the wider economic, social and political structures which account for people not being able to do or be well with the goods which are distributed. One of the key reasons for this maldistribution is very often the lack of agency of the marginalized, of those who are not able to do or be well; it is their political exclusion from the sphere of decision-making in which action to remedy their situation can be taken. Schlosberg (2009: 34) summarizes its all-embracing nature:

> The capability approach expands the distributional realm as it focuses not just on the distribution of goods we need to flourish, but the processes we depend on for that flourishing to occur. . . . Whether we can function fully is the key test of justice. Justice then is not simply about distribution, but also about all it takes – recognition, participation and more – to be able to fully live the lives we design.

A central question of environmental ethics is whether the natural environment should be valued for its own sake, independently of its potential use for humans, or only for its impact on human life. The capability approach can accommodate both an anthropocentric and biocentric interpretation (see Chapter 2). If people come to value, through democratic processes where each person contributes as social peers, that endangered species should be protected, independently of their usefulness for human life, or that nature should have rights as humans have, this is a valuable capability, even if this opportunity to function well does not belong to human beings but to animals, plants or ecosystems.

When used to assess relations between humans and the natural environment, the language of the capability approach can also accommodate within its fold elements from three major ethical theories which have divided Western philosophy, namely utilitarianism, liberalism and virtue ethics.[5] It takes the consequentialism of utilitarianism but broadens it beyond utility considerations. It assesses human actions according to their consequences for the ability of humans, and some would add ecosystems, to function well. It also borrows from (political) liberalism by situating what people should do in what they mutually agree on through public reasoning processes (for example, deciding through deliberative processes to tax environmentally damaging consumption of goods), whilst implicitly taking elements from virtue ethics by focusing on human agency, on how people act and relate to each other, in order to restore ecological balance. As Sen puts it in one of his rare writings on environmental protection, 'current environmental disaster has been created by our human actions, it is up to our actions as well to sort out the mess' (Sen 2013a: 7).

It must be noted, however, that Sen is reluctant to submit agency to the demands of the good of oneself, others and the environment. He prefers talking of 'enlightened agency', meaning a human action which has been informed by processes of public reasoning and has been submitted to the test of critical scrutiny.[6] For Sen, this 'enlightened' reasoning process is sufficient to ward off human actions which may risk being oppressive to others and to nature, as long as of course all can participate in that reasoning process as social peers, especially those who suffer because of other people's actions.

The above may sound a rather praising account of the capability approach, and one may wonder whether it can indeed be so broad ranging without losing its coherence. As a moral approach which seeks to analyse situations from the perspective of human freedom in its dual aspects of wellbeing and agency, the capability approach does not hold copyright on how these are conceptualized. This is why it can embrace many other approaches. They may not refer to the technical vocabulary of capabilities, functionings and agency, but because they take as their premises that the human person, and her flourishing as a human being – including the successful functioning of nature of which humans are part – is the end one should aim at, and that humans have the freedom to act and shape the world according to their freely chosen ends, various normative perspectives can mutually enrich each other.

The capability approach is versatile enough in adapting to its surrounding environment of analysis so as to be accommodated within religious normative frameworks. There have recently been initiatives at linking key insights of the capability approach with the Qur'an, such as the concept of 'falah' or wellbeing, which includes obligations to provide food, health, shelter, economic security and safe environment to all, respect the natural environment, ensure a fair and equitable distribution of material wealth and protect the weak from exploitation by the strong.[7] Similar research is being undertaken to link the capability approach with a Christian normative framework and its ideas of solidarity, preferential option for the poor, dignity of the human person, structural sin, forgiveness and hope.[8]

Forming speakers and agents of change

As such, the capability approach does not give a blueprint for how best to expand capabilities, for how best to provide opportunities for people to be or do what they have reason to value, and for how best to define the valuable beings and doings to be given opportunities for. That human beings are agents of their own lives and shape, through free action, their lives and the world around them is the most basic characteristic trait of the normative language that has been described in this book. But agency does not come out of nowhere. One is not born an agent. One becomes an agent through interaction with others. It is through processes of recognition by others that one acquires the necessary conditions to become an agent of change in one's own life, the life of others and in the natural world.

Borrowing from the work of Axel Honneth, Pereira (2013: 19) argues that there are three domains in which people need to be recognized by others so they may become agents: (1) the domain of intimate and close relationships where people acquire self-trust (people need to be recognized for who they are so they are able to understand their own needs); (2) the domain of legal relationships where people acquire self-respect (people need to be recognized as equal subjects of rights so they are able to understand themselves as deserving equal treatment); (3) the domain of social relationships where people acquire self-esteem (people need to be recognized for their achievements so they are able to understand themselves as having talents and are able to contribute to the life of society). When these intimate, legal and social relationships are not functioning well, people lose the conditions for being an agent. Pereira (2013: 65) concludes that it is impossible for people to engage in public reasoning processes, that is, to argue a position on the ground of reasons, make claims or disagree with others, without having these relations to oneself of self-trust, self-esteem and self-respect which can only be acquired through interaction with others. A key aspect of social justice is therefore the transformation of the relationships which undermine the conditions for people to become agents and the establishment of relationships which enable people to be recognized as individual, legal and social subjects.

To illustrate his argument, Pereira (2013: 114–17) gives the example of three hypothetical persons, Andrés, Luis and Ana, each being a prototype of the lives of millions of Latin Americans.[9] Andrés was born in an area similar to the ones of the Argentinian *villas* described in the previous chapter. He makes a living out of recycling the material he finds on the city's dump. Today there is work and food on the table, tomorrow there may not be. Preoccupied with feeding his family on a daily basis and securing housing and the basic necessities of life, he has been unable to plan his life further ahead. His wife may work too, but her job is also insecure and not well paid, and their joint income barely allows them to be adequately sheltered and fed. They live in an area which does not have good public schools, is prone to violence and does not have decent job opportunities, but they cannot afford to live elsewhere. In the absence of other opportunities, their children are highly likely to reproduce the day-to-day subsistence living of their parents.

Luis lives in the same area but is a carpenter. His father opened a carpentry workshop and he has learned the craft of making furniture at home. Thanks to some vocational training given by civil society organizations, he has been able to obtain a technical secondary education, and has expanded his workshop, hiring a few young people and training them in woodcraft. Thanks also to some people coming from the wealthier part of the city to volunteer in the area, he is given antique furniture to restore and will soon be able to set up a furniture restoration business. His business is profitable enough for him to live simply but decently and he is even able to start saving some money in case his children would like to pursue further education beyond the secondary level. They are already receiving private tutorials from volunteers to prepare them.

The third person is Ana. She has been working in a shoe factory from a very young age. The factory closed because its owners had other factories elsewhere and decided it was no longer profitable enough to maintain the factory in which Ana worked. With her co-workers, Ana mobilized to reclaim the factory and restart its activities under cooperative ownership. Although not well educated, Ana was able to align herself with her colleagues and create an alternative mode of production. Through the many meetings she participated in, she was able to understand the problems of a certain mode of economic production and the negative effects it had on her life and that of others. She is now often seen at public demonstrations to request stronger state regulations in financial transactions to ensure greater macro-economic stability.

Each of these three lives illustrates how different modes of relations have shaped their agency, their ability to be a 'doer' and to shape their own lives. Andrés has very little access to relations which will give him self-trust, self-respect and self-esteem. He may have grown up in an abusive household and might have suffered from domestic violence as a child. He has not been recognized by his close relationships in his needs and has not learned how to express them, for they were cut short by fear. He is not recognized as an equal subject of rights as he is not receiving the same treatment by state authorities – his access to public services is limited by the very fact of living where he lives. He has little self-esteem as he is not recognized as contributing to society, for his job as rubbish-recycler is not socially valued. In such a relational context, it is difficult for Andrés to start reflecting on his life and to question the economic, social and political reality which keeps him in a permanent state of poverty and social exclusion. He has never acquired the confidence to speak up for his needs (lack of self-trust), he is not seen as an equal subject of rights as he is not treated the same way by public authorities (lack of self-respect), and he is not valued by society (lack of self-esteem). In contrast, Luis exercises a profession, which gives him self-esteem. He grew up in an intimate environment – family relations and school friendships – which gave him self-trust. He may live in the same area as Andrés but his job of restoring antique furniture links him with people outside who treat him as any craftsman and this gives him a sense of self-respect. These conditions gave him the necessary confidence to expand his business and hire workers. Ana too has, through her friendships with co-workers, gained the self-trust to recognize her own needs and dignity and was able to engage, with others, in a critical reflection about which mode of economic production best secured dignified work. Even if working on a factory-line did not give her much self-esteem as such, together with others, she felt part of an economic project which was socially valued, and she was proud of her contribution to the activities of the enterprise as a whole.

Thus, 'speaking the capability approach', in the sense of acting and participating in the life of society (agency) so that each person can be given opportunities to do or be what he or she has reason to value on a shared planet (wellbeing) requires the formation of speakers. It requires establishing the necessary relationships which will actually enable people to become agents of their own lives, raise their voices, express their suffering and take actions to change the state of affairs so that opportunities for valuable sets of beings and doings may be expanded. To take back Sen's analogy of the ill-fitting shoe (Sen 2013b), if an economic, social or political structure is making a human being suffer, it is the relationships that a person has with others which will enable him or her to express his or her suffering and act towards ending the suffering. Before being remedied, suffering first has to be *recognized* by others.

Social movements play here a critical role in (1) establishing the relationships where people will acquire self-trust, self-respect and self-esteem so that they can express the suffering they endure from not having opportunities to be or do what they have reason to value; and (2) in having these sufferings recognized so that their economic, social and political causes can be removed. The next section illustrates this in the case of the social movement for the health of La Oroya, which has already been referred to in the previous chapter.

Being agents of change in the struggles for wellbeing

Rosa Amaro resides in the old city of La Oroya, and lives near the smelter. She is the President of the Movement for the Health of La Oroya (MOSAO, or Movimiento por la Salud de La Oroya), a social movement, which has been key in getting the contamination of the city and its health damage on the public agenda. When her five-year-old son was discovered to have lead levels in his blood five times higher than the safe level recommended by the

World Health Organization, she became a very active member of the movement to demand that the people of La Oroya be recognized in their sufferings and be given opportunities to be and do what they have reason to value: live a healthy life and enjoy blue skies instead of having their lives blighted by health problems caused by pollution and seeing a permanent grey cloud over the city.[10] In what follows, the origin and activities of the movement will be described, emphasizing two points: the critical role of relationships in the formation of agency, and the struggles, and conflicts, that acting in view of creating opportunities to be or do what people have reason to value, involve. All information in this section is taken from Scurrah *et al.* (2009).

Until the early 1990s, there had been no environmental awareness in the city of La Oroya. People saw animals dying, their plants not growing the way they should, but these events never led to the problem of contamination being recognized and put on the policy agenda. People were not acting to do something about it. There was a taboo about the problem, as it was feared that, should it be recognized, the smelter would close down and people would lose their jobs. Things started to change in the 1990s when some Peruvian NGOs, especially CooperAcción and Red Uniendo Manos Perú, and the international NGO Oxfam America, organized workshops with the local population about the contamination problems of the city. The personal relationships created by these gatherings gave the local population self-trust in speaking out about their problems. The involvement of Lima-based and international NGOs broke their sense of exclusion in front of public authorities and helped them gain self-respect and recognition that they were legal subjects of the state of Peru, and therefore entitled to be granted the right to live a healthy life. These workshops, facilitated by actors external to the community, led local people to form an 'Association of Environmental Delegates'.

One of their first actions was to organize an exhibition of animals that were sick or deformed because of pollution. One could say that this action may have given them a sense of self-esteem, a sense of contributing to society and doing something meaningful by publicly expressing the problem of pollution and its consequence on natural life. But this action also led to some conflict. The smelter company was quick to react to the exhibition by giving free medication for the animals in an attempt to make people believe that animals were sick because of lack of medication and not because of the contamination, and by mistreating people who went to see the exhibition. This intimidation of the company and unionized smelter workers who feared that environmental activism threatened their jobs would be a constant feature accompanying the actions of any agent acting to create opportunities for people to live healthy lives in La Oroya, some being physically attacked on the streets, some receiving abusive anonymous phone calls and some even receiving death threats.[11]

After the animal exhibition, the local NGOs and the Association for Environmental Delegates were keen to commission a scientific study which would provide clear evidence of the contamination and its effect on people's health. Lead poisoning was a specific concern but no study of lead levels in people's blood had been conducted so far. Oxfam America stepped in to support such a study and also suggested the creation of a 'movement for the health of La Oroya', which would gather all grassroots organizations concerned with the health damage caused by the smelter activities. Among these were the Committee of Neighbourhood Boards, the Human Rights Committee of the Parish of La Oroya and the Oroya Chamber of Commerce. In 2001, Oxfam America organized a workshop to discuss the desirability of establishing such a movement. The participants of the workshop decided that such a movement should be formed but that NGOs would only have an advisory and technical expertise so as not to dominate or interfere. They would step in only when the people of La Oroya wanted them to do so. The aim of the movement was to raise awareness of the environmental problem of La Oroya and hold the smelter company and the Peruvian state responsible for the pollution.

The Peruvian NGO, Red Uniendo Manos ('Joining Hands against Poverty Network), was funded by the US Presbyterian Church, and in the US it mobilized in Missouri, where the owner of the La Oroya smelter, Doe Run, had another company which had been causing environmental problems too. American journalists wrote newspaper articles and made documentaries about La Oroya, which led to the contamination problems being recognized internationally. This international recognition prompted the Peruvian media to start talking about the issue too. As a consequence of this increase in self-respect, to refer to Honneth/Pereira's analysis, MOSAO members gained the confidence to launch a legal suit against the Peruvian state to provide health care for people suffering from lead poisoning, and brought the La Oroya case to the Inter-American Human Rights Commission. MOSAO members were also extremely active in pressuring the government, in its Ministry for Energy and Mines, not to grant the extension that the smelter company was asking for in order to comply with its environmental obligations. They gained inclusion in meetings held between the Ministry and the company. But despite these actions, they failed in preventing the government from granting the company more leeway in its compliance of regulations. Their only success has been in making the government concede a shorter extension than the one initially requested.

After this relative failure to hold the company responsible for cleaning up its polluting activities, the movement weakened. This was not only due to a loss in motivation given these setbacks but also conflict from within the movement. The local Catholic church, especially as represented by the figure of the archbishop of Huancayo, played a large role in the public profile of MOSAO, but, on the accusation of improper mixing of clerics with politics, the Lima-based cardinal put pressure on the local church to withdraw from MOSAO, and local clergy was replaced with a less socially and politically active one. Many MOSAO members suffered abuse and threats which undermined their motivation to be engaged in the movement. There were also changes of staff in the local and international NGOs, which did not help in maintaining good relationships with the grassroots organizations of La Oroya.

This book has argued that wellbeing and agency were the two keywords of the language of the capability approach, and that 'public reasoning' was the verb which gave the language its dynamic. But it is relationships which hold these words and verb together. In the case of securing the wellbeing of people in La Oroya, and their capability to live healthy lives specifically, relationships between the inhabitants and Peruvian and international NGO staff were critical. Without these, there would most probably have been no identification and recognition of the sufferings of the inhabitants. The Catholic and Presbyterian churches played a significant role in not only pastoral support at the local level but also at building solidarity links between the Missouri town where Doe Run, the smelter company owner, had its headquarters, and La Oroya. Without these relationships, the inhabitants of La Oroya would not have become agents of their own lives and engaged in 'public reasoning processes' through protest, media intervention, dialogue with government officials and other ways, so that they could be or do what they had reason to value.

The capability approach has tended to be divided into so-called 'individualist' and 'collective' interpretations (see Chapter 2). The La Oroya story supersedes that division by highlighting that the 'collective' is always mediated by inter-subjective relations (Pereira 2013: 145). MOSAO was indeed an example of 'collective action', an action which could only happen through the joint efforts of the inhabitants of La Oroya, who together created something bigger than their own individual actions could do and therefore achieved what no single individual could do on his or her own. But MOSAO was mediated through interpersonal relationships. When these change, so does the movement. When NGO staff and local Catholic clergy were replaced, the movement significantly weakened in its cohesion and actions. The movement is an agent of change not because it is a collective body but because it is a set of relationships between people who together form more than their parts.

This chapter has focused on a very local social movement to illustrate how the forming and speaking of a normative language founded on wellbeing and agency works in practice. There are hundreds of thousands of other similar movements, at local, national or global level, through which persons have become agents of social change and are acting to create opportunities for people to live well.[12] Their actions have often taken the form of struggles, for they unavoidably confront the reality of unjust structures, which are built on unjust relationships of domination and exploitation. And the people who sustain these unjust relations are not always eager to readily give up their position of privilege and power.

The members of MOSAO had to confront a political structure characterized by a long history of domination by international investors and little concern for recognizing the sufferings of those whose wellbeing was being undermined by these investments. Within such a structure, it is difficult for elected political leaders to change the mode of political relationships and make them more accountable and less exploitative, and transform them so that they enable people to be or do what they have reason to value. MOSAO members tried to change the political structure, through bringing their concern into the national and international media, and gain a voice in the discussion between the Ministry for Energy and Mines and the smelter company. Those who within the structure were willing to transform it often had to endure costs – the government representative who allowed them to participate in meetings was forced to resign as a consequence. There was also confrontation with those who gain in reproducing an economic structure which submits human lives and nature to the objective of profits. The smelter company used intimidation and divisive tactics to maintain the exploitative economic relationships on which it is built.

Amaryta Sen has created a moral approach to see the world from the perspective of human freedom, in its dual aspects of wellbeing and agency. Obviously, the world did not have to wait for the 'capability approach' to appear on the academic scene in the early 1980s to provide an analytical framework with which to judge situations from the perspective of freedom and to transform them if these situations were obstructing the ability of people to live a life they had reason to choose and value. The social movement for the abolition of slavery in the nineteenth century did not need the capability approach to articulate that slavery was an unjust situation depriving human beings of their freedom, stripping both their wellbeing and agency, and that action was needed to transform that situation. Nor did the suffragette social movement need the capability approach to articulate that women were equally entitled to participate in political life by virtue of their shared humanity with men.

People may articulate their sufferings and struggles to end them through a variety of normative languages, whether religious or secular. The capability approach provides a common language, whatever one's ideological, religious or cultural background, with which to speak and narrate the stories of people who strive to live well on a shared planet. By speaking the language of 'freedom', it can speak to the dominant narrative framework of current global economic and political arrangements, but radically rethinks and reshapes the meaning of freedom altogether. And by doing so, it fundamentally questions the very project of development.

Notes

1 For an overview of different feminist theories, including liberal feminism, see Bryson (2003).
2 See for example Okin Moller (1989), who argued that because the family is the primary institution of formative moral development, justice concerns apply not only to relations between citizens but also to family members.
3 Bryson (2003: 160ff.) characterizes radical feminism as feminist political theories which give voice to women's own experiences of oppression, consider oppression of women as the most fundamental and universal form of domination, and see patriarchy, defined as a *system* of male domination, as central to that oppression.
4 See also Jaggar (2006) for a critique of (Western) liberal feminists and their tendency to deny the voices of oppressed women themselves and to ignore their own participation in an economic and political system, which undermines women's lives in the global South.
5 For a summary of the many approaches to environmental ethics and justice, and how the capability approach links to them, see Armstrong (2013).
6 Oral communication during a talk on 'The Discovery of Women', Sheldonian Theatre, University of Oxford, 7 June 2013. When asked if his reference to 'enlightened agency' was another word for 'agency for the common good', Sen reiterated his non-subscription to the idea of the common good for this would be at odds with what people freely agree on – however this concern need not be, for what constitutes the common good is constantly deliberated and questioned (see Chapter 3). The idea of 'enlightened agency' is also discussed in Drèze and Sen (2013) in relation to women's agency to overcome women's oppression. They characterize 'enlightened' or 'informed critical' agency as the 'freedom to question established values and traditional priorities' (Drèze and Sen 2013: 232).
7 The document 'Human Development in Islam' is not yet publicly available. Some background documents can be accessed at http://www.islamic-relief.com/indepth.
8 Most of this work is currently in the form of doctoral research and is not yet available publicly.
9 The stories have been slightly modified and expanded from the ones given in Pereira (2013).
10 For a short account of her life, see http://es.oxfamamerica.org/tag/movimiento-por-la-salud-de-la-oroya, and the video link therein (in Spanish only).

11 A doctor who tried to collect evidence of lead levels in newborn babies testified that he had to collect the blood clandestinely for fear of reprisals. See the interview in the video about Rosa Amaro in note 10, above.
12 For a discussion of such movements which are reshaping economic and political structures so as to orient them towards providing the conditions for each to live well on a shared planet, see de Sousa Santos (2007a, b).

CONCLUSION

Many policies have been undertaken under the banner of development. This book has discussed a few of them. The tax breaks and other incentives given to foreign investors in the Ica valley of Peru and which have created the asparagus boom have indeed generated more aggregate income for the region, but it has also contributed to depleting water resources. The building of dams in Panama, facilitated by the Clean Development Mechanism scheme, is generating more electricity so as to fuel more energy-intensive economic activities and raising the general level of income of the country, but it is destroying a rich and fragile ecosystem and dispossessing people of their land. India as a whole is generating more income than ever in its history, yet half of its children still suffer from malnutrition.

There has been a lot of unease with the very idea of development and what has been done under its name. 'Human development' was an attempt to humanize the processes of economic and social change and ensure that humans, and their flourishing, were at their centre. But an increasingly large number of scholars and social activists are calling to discard the word 'development' from the policy and social sciences vocabulary.[1] The capability approach is said to have laid the foundations of 'human development' by providing a framework with which to assess whether people's lives were flourishing or not in the economic processes of accumulation. Development was about expanding the 'real wealth of nations', that is, the opportunities people have to live long, healthy and creative lives. This book has argued that the capability approach has gone beyond 'human development' and is providing conceptual contents to a development-free or 'post-development' world. With its core concepts of wellbeing and agency, it has shifted the development discourse from development to justice. The question is not whether countries are more or less developed than others but whether societies are more just or unjust than others. The capability approach gives a framework for assessing how just societies are and how to make them less unjust.

This book started with discussing the need to recover the normative foundation of development. Through some policy case studies, Chapter 1 highlighted the many normative questions which development policies raised. How should a society move into the future? How should people live? How to distribute the costs and benefits that certain policies may entail? Who has legitimate power to make policy decisions? How should humans relate to the natural environment? The chapter argued that these questions were inescapable and that a normative framework which could provide the tools to answer these questions was needed. The next two chapters then presented the capability approach as a normative language which may help narrate these socio-economic situations which the first chapter described.

Chapter 2 unpacked its key concepts of wellbeing and agency and emphasized the need for interpretation so as to use the language in a variety of situations for a variety of purposes. While initially designed as an assess-ment framework to judge states of affairs from the perspective of people's freedom – whether they are able to do or be what they have reason to value and are able to be agents of their own lives, it argued that, by judging situations, the language also had a transformative aspect. When situations are judged as not giving opportunities for people to be or do what they have reason to value, what the language calls 'capabilities' and what the chapter interpreted as 'opportunities for living well', there is an implicit moral injunction to transform these situations so that people may live better human lives. This transformation required a certain form of action.

Chapter 3 discussed the relationship between wellbeing and justice and how the capability approach presented an idea of justice. It contended that there was a close connection between the opportunities people had to live well and the type of relationships they had with one another, and in particular how they exercised agency and acted towards each other and their natural environment. Whether people have opportunities to live a life they have reason to value critically depends on how justly they acted towards each other. The chapter defined 'just actions' as those oriented towards the creation of opportunities for all to live well on a shared planet, and it discussed the relationship between just actions and just economic, social and political structures.

In Chapter 4, two realities were analysed using the language of the capability approach in its above interpretation: the marginal urban areas of Buenos Aires in Argentina, and the smelter town of La Oroya in Peru. It centred on two methodological steps of analysis: (1) an assessment or judgement of the situation from the perspective of people's capabilities: Are people in these situations able to be or do what they have reason to value?; (2) an assessment of the economic, social and political structures: Are social actors acting justly? On the basis of this, the chapter examined how the capability approach could help in shaping transformative action so that people may enjoy certain valuable capabilities. It put special focus on the transformation of unjust structures.

The final chapter discussed how this normative language, which takes the perspective of freedom in its dual aspects of wellbeing and agency, could be acquired and spoken by social actors. It emphasized the non-ownership that the capability approach has on its keywords, and its ability to embrace a wide ideological and religious spectrum which shares similar concerns for human freedom. Regarding the formation of people who speak the moral language of wellbeing and agency, the chapter underlined the critical importance of relationships which constitute the very conditions for agency. It is through interaction with others that we may become agents of our own lives and of the world around us. It illustrated this in the case of the social movement for health in La Oroya.

There are numerous other cases of the capability approach in action, of cases where people have become agents so as to create opportunities for living well. What this book has set out to do is present a language with which these stories can be articulated. This language is a freedom-based language, but its founder has left the interpretation of freedom purposively vague and ambiguous. The interpretation this book gave proposes an understanding of freedom in the form of living well and acting justly. Sometimes, the exercise of one's freedom may undermine the opportunities other people have to enjoy a set of valuable beings and doings, such as having one's voice heard or being adequately fed and sheltered. Some managers and workers of the smelter company of La Oroya used their freedom to intimidate and abuse the environmental activists. Some inhabitants of the Argentinian *villa* used their freedom to bribe governmental officials to get the best business deals for themselves and leave others empty handed. Freedom may go astray and unjust situations result from it, but as Sen has repeatedly argued, the remedy does not lie in less, but in more freedom. We are left free as to how to use our freedom to shape our own lives, that of others and the natural environment. Whether we use our freedom 'well' is for each of us to ponder and deliberate together. This first book in the

Human Development and Capability Debates series hopes to have made a small contribution to this deliberation.

Note

1   See especially the writings of Arturo Escobar and Gilbert Rist. A brief summary can be found in Rist (2010).

GLOSSARY

Agency   The ability people have to pursue goals that they have reason to value (whether connected to their own or other people's wellbeing, including ecological balance). Agency also relates to the degree of involvement of a person in the decisions which affect his or her life.

Capabilities   Opportunities people have to achieve certain functionings.

Capabilities people have reason to value: The functionings people have agreed on, through processes of public reasoning, as being important to be given opportunities for in their specific context.

Central human capabilities: The functionings which are characteristic of good human living and which everyone are to be given opportunities for.

Capabilities approach   A moral approach to assess and judge (and transform) realities from the perspective of central human capabilities.

Capability approach   A moral approach to assess and judge (and transform) realities from the perspective of human freedom, in its dual aspects of wellbeing and agency.

Development ethics   The academic field of inquiry concerned with the meaning of processes of social change. It involves a critical reflection about the ends these processes seek to pursue and the means chosen to purse these ends.

Functionings   Beings and doings, or states of existence and activities, which characterize how well a human being functions.

Injustice   A situation is unjust if people who are living in it are unable to be or do what they have reason to value (Sen's interpretation), or unable to achieve central human functionings (Nussbaum's interpretation).

Justice   The process of transformation from an unjust situation to a less unjust situation. In other words, the process of removal of the obstacles which prevent people from doing and being what they have reason to value (Sen's interpretation), or which deprive people of opportunities to achieve central human functionings (Nussbaum's interpretation).

Public reasoning   Processes of dialogue and discussion for deciding on certain courses of action, and in which listening to divergent points of views and seeing the world from another person's perspective are essential.

Structural injustice   A situation is structurally unjust if people who are living in it relate to each other in economic exchange, social encounter or public decision-making in a way which undermines their own or other people's wellbeing and agency.

Unjust structures   What structures human interaction at the economic, social, political and cultural level in a way which undermines wellbeing and agency.

Wellbeing   The ability people have to function well as human beings, or opportunities people have to do or be what they have reason to value (Sen's interpretation), or to achieve central human functionings (Nussbaum's interpretation).

BIBLIOGRAPHY

Albó, X. (2008) 'Buen vivir = Convivir bien', *CIPCA Notas* 217, Centro de Investigación y Promoción del Campesinado, February, at http://cipca.org.bo.

Alexander, J. M. (2010) 'Ending the liberal hegemony: Republican freedom and Amartya Sen's theory of capabilities', *Contemporary Political Theory*, 9(1): 5–24.

Alkire, S. (2002) *Valuing Freedoms*, Oxford University Press, Oxford.

—— (2005) 'Why the capability approach', *Journal of Human Development*, 6(1): 115–33.

—— (2008a) 'Choosing dimensions: The capability approach and multidimensional poverty', in N. Kakwani and J. Silber (Eds), *The Many Dimensions of Poverty*, Palgrave, Basingstoke, pp. 89–119.

—— (2008b) 'Using the capability approach: Prospective and evaluative analyses', in S. Alkire, M. Qizilbash and F. Comim (Eds), *The Capability Approach: Concepts, Measures and Applications*, Cambridge University Press, Cambridge, pp. 26–50.

—— and Santos, M-E. (2013) 'A multidimensional approach: Poverty measurement and beyond', *Social Indicators Research*, 112(2): 239–58.

Arendt, H. (1958) *The Human Condition*, Chicago University Press, Chicago.

Armstrong, A. (2013) *Ethics and Justice for the Environment*, Routledge, London.

Bagchi, A. K. (2000) 'Freedom and development as end of alienation', *Economic and Political Weekly*, (9 December): 4409–20.

Ballet, J., Dubois J-L. and Mahieu, F-R. (2007) 'Responsibility for each other's freedom: Agency as the source of collective capability', *Journal of Human Development*, 8(2): 185–201.

Bebbington, A. and Bebbington-Humphreys, D. (2011) 'An Andean avatar: Post-neoliberal and neoliberal strategies for securing the unobtainable', *New Political Economy*, 15(4): 131–45.

Becker, G. (1993) 'Nobel Lecture: The economic way of looking at behaviour', *Journal of Political Economy*, 101(3): 385–409.

Biswas-Diener, R. and Diener, E. (2001) 'Making the best of a bad situation: Satisfaction in the slums of Calcutta', *Social Indicators Research*, 55(3): 329–52.

Blackledge, P. and Knight, K. (Eds) (2011) *Virtue and Politics: Alasdair MacIntyre's Revolutionary Aristotelianism*, University of Notre Dame Press, Notre Dame, IN.

Boni, A. and Walker, M. (Eds) (2013) *Human Development and Capabilities: Re-Imagining the University of the Twenty-First Century*, Routlege, London.

Borras, S. M. (2010) 'La Via Campesina and its global campaign for agrarian reform', in S. M. Borras, M. Edelman and C. Kay (Eds), *Transnational Agrarian Movements Confronting Globalization*, Blackwell, Oxford, pp. 91–121.

Brighouse, H. and Robeyns, I. (Eds) (2010) *Measuring Justice*, Cambridge University Press, Cambridge.

Bruni, L., Comim, F. and Pugno, M. (Eds) (2008) *Capabilities and Happiness*, Oxford University Press, Oxford.

Bryson, Valérie (2003) *Feminist Political Theory: An Introduction*, Palgrave, Basingstoke.

Chari, S. and Corbridge, S. (2008) *The Development Reader*, Routledge, London.

Clark, D. A. (Ed.) (2012) *Adaptation, Development and Poverty: The Dynamics of Subjective Wellbeing*, Palgrave, Basingstoke.

—— (Ed.) (2013) 'Book symposium on creating capabilities', *Journal of Human Development and Capabilities*, 14(1): 155–88.

Cowen, M. P. and Shenton, R. W. (1996). *Doctrines of Development*, Routledge, London.

Crocker, D. (2006) 'Sen and deliberative democracy', in A. Kaufmann (Ed.), *Capabilities Equality: Basic Issues and Problems*, Routledge, New York, pp. 155–97.

—— (2008) *Ethics of Global Development: Agency, Capability, and Deliberative Democracy*, Cambridge University Press, Cambridge.

Cruces, G. and Gasparini, L. (2009) 'Desigualdad en Argentina: Una revisión de la evidencia empírica', *Desarrollo Económico*, 48(192): 395–437; and 49(193): 3–29.

Dean, H. (2009) 'Critiquing capabilities: The distractions of a beguiling concept', *Critical Social Policy*, 29(2): 261–78.

Deneulin, S. (2008) 'Beyond individual agency and freedom: Structures of living together in the capability approach', in S. Alkire, M. Qizilbash and F. Comim (Eds), *The Capability Approach: Concepts, Measures and Applications*, Cambridge University Press, Cambridge, pp. 105–24.

—— (Ed.) (2009) *An Introduction to the Human Development and Capability Appraoch*, Earthscan, London.

—— and Townsend, N. (2007) 'Public goods, global public goods and the common good', *International Journal of Social Economics*, 34(1–2): 19–36.

——, Sagovsky, N. and Nebel, M. (Eds) (2006) *Transforming Unjust Structures: The Capability Approach*, Springer, Dordrecht.

Desmarais, A. (2008) 'The power of peasants: Reflections on the meanings of La Vía Campesina', *Journal of Rural Studies*, 24(2): 138–49.

de Sousa Santos, B. (Ed.) (2007a) *Another Production is Possible*, Verso, London.

—— (2007b) *Democratizing Democracy*, Verso, London.

Drèze, J. and Sen, A. (2002) *India: Development and Participation*, Oxford University Press, Delhi.

—— (2011) 'Putting growth in its place', *Outlook India*, 14 November 2011, at www.outlookindia.com.

—— (2013) *An Uncertain Glory: India and its Contradictions*, Penguin, London.

Easterlin, R. *et al.* (2010) 'The happiness-income paradox revisited', *Proceedings of the National Academy of Sciences of the United States of America*, 107(52): 22463–8.

Escobar, E. (1995) *Encountering Development*, Princeton University Press, Princeton, NJ.

Evans, P. (2002) 'Collective capabilities, culture and Amartya Sen's *Development as Freedom*', *Studies in Comparative International Development*, 37(2): 54–60.

Feldman, S. (2010) 'Social development, capabilities, and the contradictions of (capitalist) development', in S. L. Esquith and F. Gifford (Eds), *Capabilities, Power and Institutions*, Pennsylvania State University Press, University Park, PA, pp. 121–41.

Finer, M. *et al.* (2009) 'Ecuador's Yasuní biosphere reserve: A brief modern history and conservation challenges', *Environment Research Letters*, 4(3): 1–15.

Finley-Brook, M. and Thomas, C. (2011) 'Renewable energy and human rights violations: Illustrative cases from indigenous territories in Panama', *Annals of the Association of American Geographers*, 101(4): 863–72.

Fraser, N. (2008) *Scales of Justice: Re-Imagining Political Space in a Globalising World*, Polity Press, Cambridge.

Frey, B. (2008) *Happiness: A Revolution in Economics*, MIT Press, Cambridge, MA.

Gasper, D. (2004) *The Ethics of Development*, Edinburgh University Press, Edinburgh.

—— (2008) 'Denis Goulet and the project of development ethics', *Journal of Human Development*, 9(3): 453–74.

—— (2012) 'Development ethics: What? Why? How?', *Journal of Global Ethics*, 8(1): 117–35.

—— and St Clair, A. (Eds) (2010) *Development Ethics*, Ashgate, London.

Gore, Ch. (2000) 'The rise and fall of the Washington consensus as a paradigm for developing countries', *World Development*, 28(5): 789–804.

Gough, I. and McGregor, J. A. (Eds) (2007) *Wellbeing in Developing Countries: From Theory to Research*, Cambridge University Press, Cambridge.

Goulet, D. (1971) *The Cruel Choice*, Atheneum, New York.

—— (1995) *Development Ethics: A Guide to Theory and Practice*, Zed Books, London.

—— (1997) 'Development ethics: A new discipline', *International Journal of Social Economics*, 24(11): 1160–71.

—— (2006) *Development Ethics at Work: Explorations 1960–2002*, Routledge, London.

Gudynas, E. (2011a) 'Good life: Germinating alternatives to development', *America Latina en Moviemento*, issue 462, February 2011, at http://www.alainet.org/active/48054.

—— (2011b), 'Buen vivir: Today's tomorrow', *Development*, 54(4): 441–7.

Hettne, B. (2009) *Thinking about Development*, Zed Books, London.

Hollenbach, D. (2002) *The Common Good and Christian Ethics*, Cambridge University Press, Cambridge.

Ibrahim, S. (2013) 'Collective capabilities: What are they and why are they important?', in *Maitreyee* 22, e-bulletin of the Human Development and Capability Association, at www.hd-ca.org.

Jaggar, A. (2006) 'Saving Amina: Global justice for women and inter-cultural dialogue', *Ethics and International Affairs*, 19(3): 55–75.

Jameson, K. (2011) 'The indigenous movement in Ecuador: The struggle for a plurinational state', *Journal of Latin American Perspectives*, 38(1): 63–73.

Keys, M. (2006) *Aquinas, Aristotle and the Promise of the Common Good*, Cambridge University Press, Cambridge.

Layard, R. (2005) *Happiness: Lessons from a New Science*, Allen Lane, London.

Lee Van Cott, D. (2005) *From Movements to Parties in Latin America: The Evolution of Ethnic Politics*, Cambridge University Press, Cambridge.

Lépore, E., Lépore, S., Mitchell, A., Macció, J. and Rivero, E. (Eds) (2012) *Capacidades de Desarrollo y Sociedad Civil en las Villas de la Ciudad*, Universidad Católica Argentina, Buenos Aires.

Lépore, S. (2012) 'Sociabilidad e integación social en las villas de Bajo Flores y de Barracas', in E. Lépore, S. Lépore, A. Mitchell, J. Macció and E. Rivero (Eds), *Capacidades de Desarrollo y Sociedad Civil en las Villas de la Ciudad*, Universidad Católica Argentina, Buenos Aires, pp. 205–68.

Lompo, K. and Trani, J-F. (2013) 'Does corporate social responsibility contribute to human development in developing countries? Evidence from Nigeria', *Journal of Human Development and Capabilities*, 14(2): 241–65.

Macció, J. and Lépore, E. (2012) 'Las villas en la ciudad de Buenos Aires. Fragmentación espacial y segmentación de las condiciones sociales de vida', in E. Lépore, S. Lépore, A. Mitchell, J. Macció and E. Rivero (Eds), *Capacidades de Desarrollo y Sociedad Civil en las Villas de la Ciudad*, Universidad Católica Argentina, Buenos Aires, pp. 43–114.

Martínez-Alier, J. *et al.* (2010) 'Sustainable de-growth: Mapping the context, criticisms and future prospects of an emergent paradigm', *Ecological Economics*, 69: 1741–7.

Martínez-Torres, M. E. and Rosset, P. (2010) 'La Vía Campesina: The birth and evolution of a transnational social movement', *The Journal of Peasant Studies*, 37(1): 149–75.

McGillivray, M. (Ed.) (2006) *Human Wellbeing: Concept and Measurement*, Palgrave, Basingstoke.

Mitchell, A. (2012) 'Las organizaciones de la sociedad civil en las villas de Bajo Flores y Barracas', in E. Lépore, S. Lépore, A. Mitchell, J. Macció and E. Rivero (Eds), *Capacidades de Desarrollo y Sociedad Civil en las Villas de la Ciudad*, Universidad Católica Argentina, Buenos Aires, pp. 115–87.

Moore, J. and Velasquez, T. (2012) 'Sovereignty negotiated: Anti-mining movements, the state and multinational companies under Correa's "21st century socialism"', in A. Bebbington (Ed.), *Social Conflict, Economic Development and Extractive Industry*, Palgrave, Basingstoke, pp. 112–33.

Naim, M. (2000) 'Fads and fashion in economic reforms: Washington consensus or Washington confusion', *Third World Quarterly*, 21(3): 505–28.

Nussbaum, M. (1988) 'Nature, function and capability: Aristotle on political distribution', *Oxford Studies in Ancient Philosophy*, Supplementary Volume, pp. 145–84.

—— (1990) 'Aristotelian social democracy', in B. Douglass *et al.* (Eds) *Liberalism and the Good*, Routledge, London, pp. 203–52.

—— (1992) 'Human functioning and social justice: In defense of Aristotelian essentialism', *Political Theory*, 20(2): 202–46.

—— (1993) 'Non-relative virtues: An Aristotelian approach', in M. Nussbaum and A. Sen (Eds), *The Quality of Life*, Clarendon Press, Oxford, pp. 242–69.

—— (2000) *Women and Human Development*, Cambridge University Press, Cambridge.

—— (2003) 'Capabilities as fundamental entitlements', *Feminist Economics*, 9(2–3): 33–59.

—— (2007) *Frontiers of Justice*, Belknap Press, Cambridge, MA.

—— (2011) *Creating Capabilities*, Harvard University Press, Cambridge, MA.

—— (2013) '*Creating Capabilities*: Response to the papers', *International Journal of Social Economics*, 40(7): 663–76.

—— and Sen, A. (Eds) (1993) *The Quality of Life*, Clarendon Press, Oxford.

Okin Moller, S. (1989) *Justice, Gender and the Family*, Basic Books, London.

Oosterlaken, I. and van den Hoven, J. (Eds) (2012) *The Capability Approach, Technology and Design*, Springer, Dordrecht.

Orihuela, J. C. (2012) 'The making of conflict-prone development: Trade and horizontal inequalities in Peru', *European Journal of Development Research*, 24(5): 688–705.

Pelenc, J., Lompo, M. K., Ballet, J. and Dubois, J-L. (2013) 'Sustainable human development and the capability approach: Integrating environment, responsibility and collective agency', *Journal of Human Development and Capabilities*, 14(1): 77–94.

Penz, P., Drydyk, J. and Bose, P. (Eds) (2011) *Displacement by Development: Ethics, Rights and Responsibilities*, Cambridge University Press, Cambridge.

Pereira, G. (2013) *Elements of a Critical Theory of Justice*, Palgrave, New York.

Phillips, D. (2006) *Quality of Life: Concept, Policy and Practice*, Routledge, London.

Radcliffe, S. (2012) 'Development for a postneoliberal era? Sumak Kawsay, living well and the limits to decolonisation in Ecuador', *Geoforum*, 43(2): 240–9.

Ranis, G. and Stewart, F. (2012) 'Success and failure in human development, 1970–2007', *Journal of Human Development and Capabilities*, 13(2): 167–95.

Rawls, J. (1971) *A Theory of Justice*, Oxford University Press, Oxford.

—— (1993) *Political Liberalism*, Columbia University Press, New York.

Ricoeur, P. (1981) *Hermeneutics and the Human Sciences*, ed. and trans. J. B. Thompson, Cambridge University Press, Cambridge.

Rist, G. (2009) *The History of Development*, 3rd edn, Zed Books, London.

—— (2010) 'Development as a buzzword', *Development in Practice*, 17(4–5): 485–91.

Rival, L. (2010) 'Ecuador's Yasuní-ITT initiative: The old and new value of petroleum', *Ecological Economics*, 70(2): 358–65.

—— (2012) 'Planning development futures in the Ecuadorian Amazon: The expanding oil frontier and the Yasuní-ITT initiative', in A. Bebbington (Ed.), *Social Conflict, Economic Development and Extractive Industry*, Palgrave, Basingstoke, pp. 153–71.

Robeyns, I. (2003) 'Is Nancy Fraser's critique of theories of distributive justice justified?', *Constellations*, 10(4): 538–53.

—— (2005) 'The capability approach: A theoretical survey', *Journal of Human Development*, 6(1): 93–114.

—— (2006) 'The capability approach in practice', *Journal of Political Philosophy*, 14(3): 351–76.

—— (2008) 'Sen's capability approach and feminist concerns', in S. Alkire, M. Qizilbash and F. Comim (Eds), *The Capability Approach: Concepts, Measures and Applications*, Cambridge University Press, Cambridge.

—— (2009) 'Equality and justice', in S. Deneulin (Ed.), *An Introduction to the Human Development and Capability Approach*, Earthscan, London.

Ryan, R. M. and Deci, E. L. (2000) 'Self-determination theory and the facilitation of intrinsic motivation, social development, and well-being', *American Psychologist*, 55(1): 68–78.

Sachs, W. (Ed.) (1992) *The Development Dictionary: A Guide to Knowledge and Power*, Zed Books, London.

Sandel, M. (2009) *Justice: What's the Right Thing to Do*, Allen Lane, London.

Schlosberg, D. (2009) *Defining Environmental Justice*, Oxford University Press, Oxford.

Scurrah, M., Lingán, J. and Pizarro, R. (2009) 'Case study: Jobs and health in Peru', in M. Scurrah and J. Atkinson (Eds), *Globalizing Social Justice: The Role of Non-Governmental Organizations in Bringing about Social Change*, Palgrave, Basingstoke, pp. 166–206.

Seligman, M. (2011) *Flourish: A Visionary New Understanding of Happiness and Well-being*, Free Press, New York.

Sen, Amartya (1980) 'Equality of What?', in S. McMurrin (Ed.), *Tanner Lectures on Human Values*, Cambridge University Press, Cambridge.

—— (1985) 'Well-being, agency and freedom: The Dewey lectures 1984', *Journal of Philosophy*, 82(4): 169–221.

—— (1987) *Ethics and Economics*, Oxford University Press, Oxford.

—— (1988) 'The concept of development', in H. Chenery and T. N. Srinivasan (Eds), *Handbook of Development Economics*, Elsevier, Amsterdam, pp. 9–25.

—— (1989) 'Development as capability expansion', *Journal of Development Planning*, 19: 41–58.

—— (1990) 'Justice: Means versus freedoms', *Philosophy and Public Affairs*, 19(2): 111–21.

—— (1992) *Inequality Re-examined*, Clarendon Press, Oxford.

—— (1993) 'Capability and well-being', in M. Nussbaum and A. Sen (Eds), *The Quality of Life*, Clarendon Press, Oxford, pp. 30–53.

—— (1995) 'Rationality and social choice', *American Economic Review*, 85(1): 1–24.

—— (1999) *Development as Freedom*, Oxford University Press, Oxford.

—— (2000) 'Consequential evaluation and practical reason', *Journal of Philosophy*, 97(9): 477–502.

—— (2002) *Rationality and Freedom*, Harvard University Press, Cambridge, MA.

—— (2004a) 'Capabilities, lists and public reason: Continuing the conversation', *Feminist Economics*, 10(3): 77–80.

—— (2004b) 'Why we should preserve the spotted owl', *London Review of Books*, 26(3): 10–11.

—— (2006) 'What do we want from a theory of justice?', *Journal of Philosophy*, 103(5): 215–38.

—— (2009) *The Idea of Justice*, Allen Lane, London.

—— (2013a) 'The ends and means of sustainability', *Journal of Human Development and Capabilities*, 14(1): 6–20.

—— (2013b) 'What is it like to be like a human being?', in United Nations Development Programme, *Human Development Report 2013*, at http://hdr.undp.org/en/reports/.

Stahler-Sholk, R. (2007) 'Resisting neoliberal homogenization: The Zapatista autonomy movement', *Latin American Perspectives*, 34(2): 48–63.

Thomson, B. (2011) 'Pachakuti: Indigenous perspectives, buen vivir, sumaq kawsay and degrowth', *Development*, 54(4): 448–54.

Thorp, R. (2012) 'The challenges of mining-based development in Peru', in R. Thorp, S. Battistelli, Y. Guichaoua, J. C. Orihuela and M. Paredes (Eds), *The Development Challenges of Mining and Oil*, Palgrave, Basingstoke, pp. 110–30.

Thorp, R. and Paredes, M. (2010) *Ethnicity and the Persistence of Inequality: The Case of Peru*, Palgrave, Basingstoke.

Trani, J-F., Bakhshi, P. and Rolland, C. (2011) 'Capabilities, perception of wellbeing and development effort: Some evidence from Afghanistan', *Oxford Development Studies*, 39(4): 403–26.

Tyler, C. (2006) 'Contesting the common good: T. H. Green and contemporary republicanism', in M. Dimova-Cookson and W. J. Mander (Eds), *T. H. Green: Ethics, Metaphysics and Political Philosophy*, Clarendon Press, Oxford.

United Nations Development Programme (UNDP) (1990) *Human Development Report*, at http://hdr.undp.org/en/.

—— (2010) *Human Development Report 20th Anniversary: The Real Wealth of Nations*, at http://hdr.undp.org/en/.

Ura, K., Alkire, S., Zangmo, T. and Wangdi, K. (2012) 'A short guide to Gross National Happiness Index', at http://www.grossnationalhappiness.com/wp-content/uploads/2012/04/Short-GNH-Index-final1.pdf.

Valencia, A. (2012a) *Human Rights Trade-offs in a Context of Systemic Unfreedom: Work vs. Health in the Case of the Smelter Town of La Oroya, Peru*, unpublished PhD dissertation, Faculty of Law at the University of Victoria, British Columbia, Canada.

—— (2012b) 'Human rights trade-offs in a context of systemic unfreedom: The case of the smelter town of La Oroya, Peru', *Bath Papers in International Development and Wellbeing*, BPD 15, Centre for Development Studies, University of Bath, Bath.

van Dijk, N. (2012) *Simply Happy?: Voluntary Simplicity and Subjective Wellbeing*, Master's dissertation, Bath, http://base.socioeco.org/docs/van_dijk_dissertation_nadine.pdf.

Walker, M. (2012) 'Universities and a human development ethics: A capabilities approach to curriculum', *European Journal of Education*, 47(3): 448–61.

Walsh, C. (2010) 'Development as buen vivir: Institutional arrangements and (de)colonial entanglements', *Development*, 53(1): 15–21.

White, S. (2010) 'Analysing wellbeing: A framework for development practice', *Development in Practice*, 20(2): 158–72.

Wolff, J. and De-Shalit, A. (2007) *Disadvantage*, Oxford University Press, Oxford.

—— (2013) 'On fertile functionings: A response to Martha Nussbaum', *Journal of Human Development and Capabilities*, 14(1): 161–5.

Yashar, D. (2005) *Contesting Citizenship in Latin America: The Rise of Indigenous Movements and the Post-Liberal Challenge*, Cambridge University Press, Cambridge.

INDEX

'Combining conceptual analysis and case studies, this book shows that poor people, their capabilities and agency, must be the foundations of the kind of thinking about well-being and justice that will prepare us for a "post-development" world, in which the artificial constructs of North and South are replaced by the much more tangible and universal divides between haves and have-nots.'
—Duncan Green, Oxfam International

'Within the world of development policy, there has been a very well-justified push for so-called "evidence-based policy making". However, this entails the risk of creating an illusion of "objectivity", which hides the system of ethical values behind specific prescriptions. This book does a great job of providing a solid normative framework for policy: widening the set of effective options people have to live the life they have reason to value. Many of the practical implications of such a framework are discussed in this work, which hopefully will become a reference for anyone engaged in the difficult task of policy advice.'
—Luis F. Lopez-Calva, Lead Economist and Regional Poverty Advisor, Europe and Central Asia Region, World Bank

The question of the meaning of progress and development is back on the political agenda. How to frame answers and search for new alternatives when socialism and liberalism no longer provide a satisfactory framework? This book introduces in an accessible way the capability approach, first articulated by Amartya Sen in the early 1980s. Written for an international audience, but rooted in the Latin American reality – a region with a history of movements for social justice – the book argues that the capability approach provides the most encompassing and promising ethical framework to date with which to construct action for improving people's wellbeing and reducing injustices in the world.

Comprehensive, practical and nuanced in its treatment of the capability approach, this highly original volume gives students, researchers and professionals in the field of development an innovative framing of the capability approach as a 'language' for action and provides specific examples of how it has made a difference.

Séverine Deneulin is Senior Lecturer in International Development, Department of Social and Policy Sciences, University of Bath, UK.

Cover image: © Universidad Centroamericana de Nicaragua
POLITICS/ DEVELOPMENT STUDIES/SUSTAINABILITY

an **informa** business

Routledge
Taylor & Francis Group
www.routledge.com

earthscan
from Routledge

ISBN 978-0-415-72024-3

9 780415 720243